# REWRITE

## A 21-Day Marriage Devotional

VANCE K. JACKSON, JR.

Rewrite: A 21-Day Marriage Devotional
ISBN: 978-1-7369832-0-1
Published by 5th Gen Publishing, LLC.
© 2021 Vance K. Jackson, Jr.
www.VanceKJackson.com

Printed in the United States of America. All rights reserved. No portion of this book may be reproduced, stored in a retrieval system, or transmitted in any form or by any means—electronic, mechanical, photocopy, recording, scanning, or other—except for brief quotations in critical reviews or articles, without the prior written permission of the publisher.

Scripture quotations taken from the Amplified® Bible (AMPC), Copyright © 1954, 1958, 1962, 1964, 1965, 1987 by The Lockman Foundation Used by permission. www.lockman.org

Scripture quotations from The Authorized King James Version (KJV). Rights in the Authorized Version in the United Kingdom are vested in the Crown. Reproduced by permission of the Crown's patentee, Cambridge University Press.

Scripture quotations marked (MSG) are taken from THE MESSAGE, copyright © 1993, 2002, 2018 by Eugene H. Peterson. Used by permission of NavPress, represented by Tyndale House Publishers. All rights reserved.

Scripture quotations marked (NIV) are taken from the Holy Bible, New International Version®, NIV®. Copyright © 1973, 1978, 1984, 2011 by Biblica, Inc.™ Used by permission of Zondervan. All rights reserved worldwide. www.zondervan.com The "NIV" and "New International Version" are trademarks registered in the United States Patent and Trademark Office by Biblica, Inc.™

Scripture quotations marked (NLT) are taken from the Holy Bible, New Living Translation, copyright © 1996, 2004, 2015 by Tyndale House Foundation. Used by permission of Tyndale House Publishers, Inc., Carol Stream, Illinois 60188. All rights reserved.

Library of Congress Cataloging-in-Publication Data
Library of Congress Control Number: 2021912974

## LOVE NOTE

*To my Nina,*

*You are forever my crown. Your intellect and beauty are breathtaking. Your wisdom, incomparable. I love our talks. I love our conversations.*

*From politics to theology. From business, sports, to world news. From financial affairs to arts & culture. I love the depth, breadth, and brilliance of our discussions. I enjoy you.*

*I even adore the simplicity of our silence. Whether we're listening to the symphonic crashing of ocean waves against the shore as we're reading books on the beach or staring at each other from across a crowded room. You satisfy me.*

*I cherish you and these intimate moments are forever written upon the pages of my heart. Our children will rise up to call you Blessed. I enjoy growing with you. A lifetime simply isn't enough.*

*I'm honored to lead you. I'm honored to love you. I'm honored to serve you. You're more than my wife, you are my gift and crown.*

*Thank you for your support, wisdom, advice, and counsel. You have my heart forever.*

*Forever yours,*
*Vance K. Jackson Jr.*

# TABLE OF CONTENTS

**DAY 1**
He Makes All Things New .......................... 11

**DAY 2**
Who Touched Me? ................................ 15

**DAY 3**
The King of Syria ................................ 23

**DAY 4**
Who's Your Counsel? ............................. 31

**DAY 5**
God's Redirection ................................ 35

**DAY 6**
Death and Life ................................... 41

**DAY 7**
A Good Name .................................... 47

**DAY 8**
Foul Communication Corrupts Marriages ............. 51

**DAY 9**
A Carnal Marriage ................................ 57

**DAY 10**
Old Wine ........................................ 63

**DAY 11**
Walk Together ................................... 69

**DAY 12**
A New Start ..................................... 73

**DAY 13**
What's Done in the Dark .......................... 77

**DAY 14**
Begin Again. . . . . . . . . . . . . . . . . . . . . . . . . . . . . . . . . . . . . . 81

**DAY 15**
Adultery . . . . . . . . . . . . . . . . . . . . . . . . . . . . . . . . . . . . . . . 85

**DAY 16**
The Wife of Thy Youth . . . . . . . . . . . . . . . . . . . . . . . . . . . 89

**DAY 17**
Ichabod . . . . . . . . . . . . . . . . . . . . . . . . . . . . . . . . . . . . . . . 95

**DAY 18**
The Yoke Breaker. . . . . . . . . . . . . . . . . . . . . . . . . . . . . . 105

**DAY 19**
The Lord Is My Shepherd. . . . . . . . . . . . . . . . . . . . . . . 111

**DAY 20**
Make Room. . . . . . . . . . . . . . . . . . . . . . . . . . . . . . . . . . 119

**DAY 21**
Declare Life. . . . . . . . . . . . . . . . . . . . . . . . . . . . . . . . . . 129

## Day 1

## HE MAKES
## ALL THINGS NEW

*And walk in love, as Christ also hath loved us, and hath given himself for us an offering and a sacrifice to God for a sweet-smelling savour.*

EPHESIANS 5:2 KJV

Walk in love, and let God rewrite the heart of your marriage. Let His Love flourish within the ground of your marriage. Let His Word wash over and renew the very fabric and framework of your family.

Let every word and deed reflect His Heart and Character within the borders of your home. Let your marriage serve as an offering and a sweet sacrifice to God. Choose to obey Christ and let every aspect of your marriage send up a sweet-smelling fragrance to Him.

When you surrender your marriage to God, every aspect of your marriage belongs to Him. Let the fruit of your marriage reflect the Heart and Character of God, both in private and in public. Choose to surrender to the True and Living King, and let your marriage reflect Christ in every season of your life.

Let Love become the foundation and framework of your marriage. Let His Grace, Peace, Wisdom, and Patience flow through the ground of your family. Choose to handle the heart of your spouse with grace, peace, wisdom, love, and mercy. Let your words and actions be seasoned with His Grace and Understanding.

When bitterness and offense pollutes the ground of your marriage, it serves as a hindrance that blocks the flow of God's Peace from thriving within its borders. When bitterness settles within the heart of your home, it blocks the flow of good, constant, and Godly communication between you and your spouse.

Bitterness will pervert your marital covenant. Bitterness will harden your heart and block effective communication. Bitterness blocks breakthrough and limits your relationship's potential. Bitterness will keep you enslaved to the offense or transgression of the past. Choose to forgive and keep moving forward.

Bitterness is a process. When you choose to meditate on the hurt, pain, and the offense of the past, bitterness will linger within the borders of your house and it will harden the soil of your heart. Choose to forgive. Choose to create an environment of peace. Choose to create an environment of forgiveness. Choose to create an environment of love.

Forgive freely. Choose to forgive frequently. When you forgive your spouse, it will release you from the bondage of the past. Forgiveness establishes the atmosphere for breakthrough. When the ground of your heart is cleansed from the bondage, pain, hurt, and offense of the past, your marriage is able to heal and function as God intended. Walk in love and let God rewrite your marriage.

Ephesians 5:2 AMPC declares, "And walk in love, [esteeming and delighting in one another] as Christ loved us and gave Himself up for us, a slain offering and sacrifice to God [for you, so that it became] a sweet fragrance."

Love sends up a sweet fragrance to God. Forgiveness has a fragrance. Selflessness has a fragrance. What's the fragrance of your marriage? Marriage is selfless. A Godly marriage sends up a sweet fragrance to God that's pleasing to Him. Choose to reflect His Love and Character in every aspect of your life. Choose to pattern the heart and character of your marriage after Christ.

Ephesians 5:2 NLT declares, "Live a life filled with love, following the example of Christ. He loved us and offered himself as a sacrifice for us, a pleasing aroma to God." Let God rewrite every aspect of your marriage. Surrender your heart to God and let Him breathe into the very heart and foundation of your family.

It is my prayer, as you read these words, that God leads your heart and transforms the very fabric of your marriage. I pray that generations are transformed through your submission and obedience to God.

I pray that God strengthens every aspect of your family's framework. As you surrender every part of your heart to God, I pray that your family is healed, renewed, restored, and made whole. I pray that God redirects and reconciles your heart back to Him. I pray that your marriage continually reflects His Love, Character, and Heart—in public and in private.

Only God can transform your heart. Only God can transform the infrastructure of your marriage. Only God can heal your heart. Only God can make you whole. Let God rewrite and soften every aspect of your marriage. Let God lead the heart of your marriage forever.

# COUPLES' PRAYER

Father God, in the Name of Jesus, we thank You for our marriage. Father, we surrender our hearts to You. Father, we surrender our lives to You.

Father God, in the Name of Jesus, we thank You for covering us and shielding us from the attacks of the enemy. Father, we stand in agreement and declare that through Your Son, Jesus Christ, we are made whole. Father, we declare that our family has a new generational bloodline through Your Son, Jesus Christ.

Father, we accept Jesus Christ as our Lord and Savior. We believe that He died for our sin and rose from the grave. Father, forgive us for our sin. Father, we forgive each other. Father, we forgive others that have wronged us. Father, we surrender to You.

Father, we give our lives to You. Lord, we give our hearts to You. Father, we give our marriage to You. Rewrite our story. Lord, rewrite our marriage and let our lives give You glory. Father, lead us. Father, strengthen us. We surrender to You now and forever.

In Jesus' Mighty Name. Amen.

## Day 2

# WHO TOUCHED ME?

*And a woman having an issue of blood twelve years, which had spent all her living upon physicians, neither could be healed of any, Came behind him, and touched the border of his garment: and immediately her issue of blood stanched. And Jesus said, Who touched me? When all denied, Peter and they that were with him said, Master, the multitude throng thee and press thee, and sayest thou, Who touched me? And Jesus said, Somebody hath touched me: for I perceive that virtue is gone out of me. And when the woman saw that she was not hid, she came trembling, and falling down before him, she declared unto him before all the people for what cause she had touched him, and how she was healed immediately. And he said unto her, Daughter, be of good comfort: thy faith hath made thee whole; go in peace.*

LUKE 8:43-48 KJV

The woman with the issue of blood spent twelve years searching for a remedy to heal her internal condition—no one had the answer. No one had the solution. No one had the cure. Although the manifestation of her problem appeared on the outside, in the form of blood, she was seeking to solve an internal problem in a carnal way.

Maybe you're like the woman with the issue of blood—maybe you've been searching for an answer to heal your heart. Maybe you've been searching for an answer to heal your marriage. Maybe you're like this woman who had been searching for twelve years for a solution to heal her issue. Maybe, like this woman, you've been bleeding while you were searching for answers. While this woman was searching, she was wounded. While she was searching, her emotional and financial resources were being drained.

Maybe your marriage is bleeding on the inside. Maybe the outward manifestation of your problem is a symptom of a deeper hidden issue. Maybe it's deeper. Maybe it's spiritual. Mark 5:25–34 KJV declares:

25. "And a certain woman, which had an issue of blood twelve years,"

26. "And had suffered many things of many physicians, and had spent all that she had, and was nothing bettered, but rather grew worse,"

27. "When she had heard of Jesus, came in the press behind, and touched his garment."

28. "For she said, If I may touch but his clothes, I shall be whole."

29. "And straightway the fountain of her blood was dried up; and she felt in her body that she was healed of that plague."

30. "And Jesus, immediately knowing in himself that virtue had gone out of him, turned him about in the press, and said, Who touched my clothes?"

31. "And his disciples said unto him, Thou seest the multitude thronging thee, and sayest thou, Who touched me?"

³². "And he looked round about to see her that had done this thing."

³³. "But the woman fearing and trembling, knowing what was done in her, came and fell down before him, and told him all the truth."

³⁴. "And he said unto her, Daughter, thy faith hath made thee whole; go in peace, and be whole of thy plague."

Notice, this woman with the issue of blood stated in Mark 5:27-28 KJV, "When she had heard of Jesus, came in the press behind, and touched his garment. For she said, If I may touch but his clothes, I shall be whole." When the woman heard that Jesus was passing by, she intentionally pressed her way through the crowds from behind. The crowds around Jesus were so dense that people could gain access to Him on every side. In fact, the crowds were so large and dense that the disciples could not keep track of who was touching Him.

In fact, when you read this text in its entirety, we uncover a hidden message in this woman's brief encounter with Christ. Let's examine the faith and emotional tenacity of this woman with the "issue of blood" as she pressed through the crowds and accessed Jesus.

According to Leviticus 15:19-31 KJV, under Levitical law, this woman with an "issue of blood" was considered "unclean." An "unclean" woman had to follow a specific Levitical protocol outlined in Leviticus 15:19-31 KJV. In fact, she could not touch or come into contact with others. If she would touch anyone, that person would also be considered "unclean." By Levitical law, she was ostracized and deemed an outcast.

But look at this woman's faith! She was willing to press beyond the normal Levitical protocol of the day in order to be made whole. Sometimes, you have to press beyond the norm in order to get your healing. Sometimes, you have to press beyond the crowds in order to get your supernatural deliverance. Sometimes, you have to press beyond the external noise in order to get your internal healing. Sometimes, you have to be intentional and press beyond the gossip and rumors in order to get your breakthrough.

In the Name of Jesus, I pray that you press beyond the opinions of others and seek Christ for healing. Seek Christ for healing for your marriage. Seek Christ for healing for your family. Seek Christ to heal and transform your family's bloodline. Choose to surrender to Christ. Let Christ make you whole.

According to Leviticus 15:30 KJV, this woman was socially ostracized, and under Levitical law, she was "spiritually tainted." According to Levitical law, a woman with an "issue of blood" was considered unclean until a priest cleared her and declared her clean.

Think about the emotional pressure this woman must have faced when she decided to step out on faith to press beyond the crowds, knowing that she was considered "unclean." Think about the whispers and the chatter that others were saying about her as she pressed through the crowds. Think about the physical, emotional, financial, psychological, and social barriers she had to overcome in order to reach Jesus.

Mark 5:27–28 KJV declares, "When she had heard of Jesus, came in the press behind, and touched his garment. For she said, If I may touch but his clothes, I shall be whole." There is no record that explains why she decided to touch the garment of Jesus. There were no written instructions on how to access Jesus. This woman went beyond the norm and decided that she wanted to get her healing. Sometimes, you have to press and rewrite what's normal.

Maybe, you have crowds around you, and on the outside, your

marriage "looks" fine, but on the inside, your marriage has some internal "issues," and it's bleeding from the inside out. In fact, as time passes—it's getting worse.

Maybe, you've been searching for answers and solutions in order to make your marriage whole. It is my prayer that as you pray together and read God's Word—you press for your marriage together. Choose to ignore the crowds. Ignore the whispers. Ignore the naysayers and let God rewrite every aspect of your marriage. God rewrote the story of the woman with the issue of blood, and He can rewrite your story as well. The only person who can make you whole is Jesus Christ.

Notice what happened immediately after the woman connected with Christ. Mark 5:30 KJV declares, "And Jesus, immediately knowing in himself that virtue had gone out of him, turned him about in the press, and said, Who touched my clothes?" The Amplified Version expounds upon Mark 5:30 AMPC in the following manner, "And Jesus, recognizing in Himself that the power proceeding from Him had gone forth, turned around immediately in the crowd and said, Who touched My clothes?"

The woman with the issue of blood accessed power from Jesus. Virtue had left from Jesus and flowed into the woman with the issue. Through Jesus Christ, there is virtue for your marriage. Through Jesus Christ, there is power for your marriage. Through Jesus Christ, there is power for your issues. Through Jesus, there is restoration for your family. When you pull on the power of Jesus Christ, He can make you whole. Let Christ in.

Notice, in Mark 5:30–31 AMPC, Jesus asked His disciples, "Who touched me?" His disciples then responded, "And the disciples kept saying to Him, You see the crowd pressing hard around You from all sides, and You ask, Who touched Me?" Pull on Christ. Ask God to heal you. Ask God to heal your marriage. Ask God to heal your heart. Ask God to heal your family. Ask God to make you whole. Jesus is not too busy for you. Your marriage is important to God. God is attentive to your need. Your family is important to God. Your wholeness is important to Him. Press past the obstacles and seek God.

Notice what Jesus said to the woman after she pressed past the opinions of men and religious protocol. Luke 8:48 KJV declares, "And he said unto her, Daughter, be of good comfort: thy faith hath made thee whole; go in peace." Her faith made her whole. Let your faith reach God. Surrender to Him. Let God heal you. Let God heal old wounds. Let God break generational cycles. Let God break generational scars. Let God break you free from every emotional pain, pit, and prison of the past. Let God make you whole.

Choose to trust Him. "And He said to her, Daughter, your faith (your confidence and trust in Me) has made you well! Go (enter) into peace (untroubled, undisturbed well-being)." Luke 8:48 AMPC. Be made whole.

## MY DECLARATION FOR YOUR MARRIAGE

May God bless the borders of your marriage. May God heal every aspect of your family. May God soften the ground of your heart. May He break every generational curse that's on your family's bloodline. May the Blood of Jesus Christ break every familial generational cycle.

May He heal old wounds. May He heal the heart of your family. May He restore you. May He make you whole. May He open up new doors of opportunity. May He establish you. May He keep you. May He bless your coming in and your going out. May He rewrite your story.

May He heal and reconcile your heart. May He heal every area of your life. May He heal every area of your marriage. May He heal every area of your ministry. May He increase you. May He enlarge you. May He expand your borders. May He increase your faith.

May He remove every barrier. May He remove every obstacle. May the Power of God crush every mountain that you face. May He open your womb. May He cause your home to flourish. May He cause your ideas to thrive. May He open your mind and give you witty ideas and inventions.

May He bless your finances. May He give you the faith to try again. May God rewrite your story. May God rewrite the legacy of your family. May God rewrite your entire marriage.

In Jesus' Name. Amen.

## Day 3

# THE KING OF SYRIA

*Therefore sent he thither horses, and chariots, and a great host: and they came by night, and compassed the city about. And when the servant of the man of God was risen early, and gone forth, behold, an host compassed the city both with horses and chariots. And his servant said unto him, Alas, my master! how shall we do? And he answered, Fear not: for they that be with us are more than they that be with them. And Elisha prayed, and said, Lord, I pray thee, open his eyes, that he may see. And the Lord opened the eyes of the young man; and he saw: and, behold, the mountain was full of horses and chariots of fire round about Elisha.*

2 KINGS 6:14-17 KJV

Fear not, there are more for your marriage, than are against you. God is for you. God is for your family. God's army is greater than any obstacle that stands in your way. God is on your side, and He wants your marriage to succeed. In fact, God wants your marriage to thrive. He wants every aspect of your marriage to flourish. Surrender to Him and let God rewrite your marriage—God can do the impossible.

In 2 Kings Chapter 6, the king of Syria warred against Israel, but God rewrote their story. Let's take a look at 2 Kings 6:8–14 KJV:

"Then the king of Syria warred against Israel, and took counsel with his servants, saying, In such and such a place shall be my camp. And the man of God sent unto the king of Israel, saying, Beware that thou pass not such a place; for thither the Syrians are come down. And the king of Israel sent to the place which the man of God told him and warned him of, and saved himself there, not once nor twice. Therefore the heart of the king of Syria was sore troubled for this thing; and he called his servants, and said unto them, Will ye not shew me which of us is for the king of Israel? And one of his servants said, None, my lord, O king: but Elisha, the prophet that is in Israel, telleth the king of Israel the words that thou speakest in thy bedchamber. And he said, Go and spy where he is, that I may send and fetch him. And it was told him, saying, Behold, he is in Dothan. Therefore sent he thither horses, and chariots, and a great host: and they came by night, and compassed the city about."

## EXALTED

According to Strong's Concordance, the Hebrew word for "Syria" is, "Aram" (H758), which means "Exalted." What has "exalted" itself against your family? What has "exalted" itself against your marriage? Who has exalted themselves against your marriage? Who or what is warring against your family?

Maybe, it's financial pressures. Maybe, it's the opinion of people that's weighing you down. Maybe, it's lust that's warring against your family's bloodline. Maybe, it's depression that's trying to weigh your family down. Or maybe, it's condemnation that's trying to remind you of the past. Who or what is warring against you and your family?

Remember, according to Strong's Concordance, the word "Syria" means "Exalted." When the king of Syria wars against your family, this spirit tries to exalt itself against you. Remember, in 2 Kings 6, when the king of Syria tried to attack Elisha, the king (or the oppressive spirit) tried to magnify himself against Elisha by sending his army in the middle of the night to surround Elisha in order to instill fear.

What's trying to suffocate your marriage? What's trying to magnify itself against your family? The king of Syria tried to silently attack Elisha in the middle of the night by surrounding him with his army. What's trying to attack you in the middle of the night? What's keeping you up at night? What's trying to suffocate your vision? What's trying to suffocate your family's dreams? Who's trying to intimidate you? What's trying to silently choke your destiny and suffocate the heart of your marriage?

In 2 Kings 6:8 KJV, let's examine this spiritual dynamic between the king of Syria and the children of Israel. Let's study and take note of how the king of Syria functioned. 2 Kings 6:8 KJV declares, "Then the king of Syria warred against Israel, and took counsel with his servants, saying, In such and such a place shall be my camp."

# HE TOOK COUNSEL

Notice that the king of Syria "took counsel." In other words, this evil king took counsel with other evil conspirators. One point to note about this spirit, the king of Syria, is that it tries to align and exalt itself with others in an attempt to overtake you. What's trying to "overtake" your marriage?

Maybe, it's people who have spoken ill of you or your spouse. Maybe, it's past memories that are trying to suffocate your joy. Maybe, it's offense and bitterness that's trying to choke your peace. No matter the case—just remember that the king of Syria, this spirit, tries to exalt itself in any area of your life in an attempt to stunt your destiny and your purpose. Don't let fear immobilize your destiny. Choose to walk forward in purpose. Don't let the king of Syria and his army stop you from pursuing everything that God has for you.

Ignore those who exalt themselves against your marriage. Don't exalt man's opinion over what God's Word declares concerning your marriage. Choose to fight for your marriage. Choose to defend your spouse. Choose to war together.

Ignore those who take ungodly counsel to war against you and your marriage. Walk not in the counsel of gossipers. Remember gossipers are not loyal—if they'll talk about others to you—then they will talk about you. Ignore those who whisper about the success or failure of other marriages. Ignore those who strategically align with others who set themselves against you. Remember that God is for you, and no man, no evil weapon or alliance can defeat you. Matthew 19:6 AMPC declares, "So they are no longer two, but one flesh. What therefore God has joined together, let not man put asunder (separate)."

The king of Syria wants to divide and destroy your marriage. Don't let pride exalt itself within the borders of your heart. Don't let haughtiness puff itself up within the borders of your heart and marriage. Proverbs 16:18 KJV declares, Pride goeth before destruction, and an haughty spirit before a fall." Pride destroys marriages.

What's trying to subdue your marriage? What's trying to overtake you? What's trying to exalt itself against your marriage? What's trying to war against your family, life, and destiny? Notice the latter part of 2 Kings 6:8 KJV, "Then the king of Syria warred against Israel, and took counsel with his servants, saying, In such and such a place shall be my camp."

## WHO'S YOUR COUNSEL?

Don't take counsel or align with those who attack and gossip about others. Choose to humble yourself and keep your hands clean and your heart pure. Invest in your marriage. Invest in your spouse. Speak life instead of division, defeat, and destruction. Choose to sow peace.

After the king of Syria took counsel and formed alliances with others against Elisha, notice what the king did next. In 2 Kings 6:8 KJV, he stated, ". . . In such and such a place shall be my camp." The king of Syria likes to set up snares. According to Strong's Concordance, the Hebrew word for "Snare" is "mowqesh" (H4170), which means "bait or lure." In other words, the king of Syria likes to set up "hidden attacks." This spirit does not only like to take counsel from ungodly sources—it also likes to form silent alliances in order to validate and amplify its message.

The king of Syria likes to silently "set up" camp within the walls of your marriage. Don't let anything sneak into your camp. Song of Solomon 2:15 KJV declares, "Take us the foxes, the little foxes, that spoil the vines: for our vines have tender grapes." It's the "little foxes", or the small things that sneak into your house that ultimately destroy the vine. Choose to get rid of the small "silent assassins" that try to destroy your marriage. Lust kills marriages. Pride destroys families. Rebellion dethrones authority. Don't let the "little" foxes destroy your family's harvest.

## IT'S THE SMALL FOXES

Foxes are sneaky and cunning animals. They like to dig holes in the ground and crouch down in an effort to hide and sneak upon their prey; and when they're ready to attack, they come out from hiding and pounce upon their victim. Don't let the foxes in. Don't allow lust to pounce upon your marriage. Close every open door. Surrender your heart to God and allow God to heal every area of your heart. Choose to repent. Turn to Him, and He will close the mouth of the lion, the fox, and every enemy that's trying to exalt itself against your marriage.

Choose to crush pride together. Surrender to God and let God lead and soften the ground of your heart. Choose to crush lust and the spirit of perversion together. Don't let your heart fall victim to their venomous trap—for the end is death. Choose life. Choose Christ. Choose His Way of doing things and let God rewrite the narrative of your marriage.

Choose to be led by God's Word. Choose to be led by His Counsel. The Word of God can conquer any storm. The Word of God can crush any attack of the enemy. The Word of God can heal old wounds. God's Word will always win. His Word will always prevail. In fact, look at what 2 Kings 6:8 KJV declares, "Then the king of Syria warred against Israel." According to Strong's Concordance, the word "Israel" (H3478) means "God prevails." God will always prevail. Choose to crush pride and let God's Word prevail within the walls of your marriage.

Choose to let His Word prevail and transform the framework of your house. God loves to rewrite stories. He loves to rewrite families. God loves to transform hearts and rewrite marriages—let God in and let Him rewrite the story of your family and marriage.

## COUPLES' PRAYER

Father God, in the Name of Jesus, we thank You for our marriage. Father, we surrender our hearts to You. Lord, we surrender our marriage to You. Father, we surrender our family to You.

Lord, remove anything that's not like You. Father, we choose to crush anything that we have exalted within the walls of our heart. Father, we choose to crush anything that we have exalted within the walls of our marriage.

In the Name of Jesus, we crush pride and surrender to You. Lord, make our heart a dwelling place of Your Peace, Love, Kindness, and Mercy. Father, the heart of our family surrenders to You.

Lord, expose every hidden thing that's not like You. Expose the idols that we have exalted within our hearts.

Lord, we lay aside every weight. Father, we lay aside every burden. Lord, we lay aside every ought, every sin, every mistake at Your feet. Lord, we repent and turn to You. Father, we choose to put the past behind us and move forward in You.

In Jesus' Name. Amen.

# Day 4

## WHO'S YOUR COUNSEL?

*Blessed is the man that walketh not in the counsel of the ungodly, nor standeth in the way of sinners, nor sitteth in the seat of the scornful. But his delight is in the law of the Lord; and in his law doth he meditate day and night. And he shall be like a tree planted by the rivers of water, that bringeth forth his fruit in his season; his leaf also shall not wither; and whatsoever he doeth shall prosper. The ungodly are not so: but are like the chaff which the wind driveth away. Therefore the ungodly shall not stand in the judgment, nor sinners in the congregation of the righteous. For the Lord knoweth the way of the righteous: but the way of the ungodly shall perish.*

PSALMS 1:1-6 KJV

Your counsel is critical to your family's success. The quality of your counsel is critical to your marriage's success. Who's your counsel? Who has your ear? Who has your heart? Whose advice are you listening to? Choose to surrender to God's Way of doing things. Listen to God's Counsel—His Counsel is His Word.

Notice what 2 Kings 6:8 KJV declares, "Then the king of Syria warred against Israel, and took counsel with his servants, saying, In such and such a place shall be my camp." Take note of the principle housed within this verse—ungodly kings take advice from ungodly counselors. Prideful kings fall and self-exalted kingdoms crumble. 1 Peter 5:6 KJV declares, "Humble yourselves therefore under the mighty hand of God, that he may exalt you in due time." The king of Syria thought that his way was better. The king of Syria exalted himself against Israel. Don't exalt yourself against God's Word.

Husbands, choose to submit to God's Word. Choose to submit to God's Way of doing things. Couples, choose to submit to one another and let God lead your marriage. Wives, submit to God. Submit to your husband. Submit one to another. Choose to surrender to God as a family. Submit to God's Way of doing things and let God lead you. Let God lead your heart. Let God lead the course of your marriage.

Notice, in 2 Kings 6:9 KJV, the Bible outlines the reward of following Godly counsel, "And the man of God sent unto the king of Israel, saying, Beware that thou pass not such a place; for thither the Syrians are come down." Elisha directed and advised the king of Israel and showed him how to navigate around the trap of the enemy. When you follow Godly counsel and the counsel of God-led mentors, advisors, and instructors, you'll avoid falling victim to the enemy's traps, snares, and pitfalls.

In 2 Kings 6:9 KJV, God used Elisha to advise the king of Israel about the enemy's plan. Elisha, who was God-led Counsel, exposed the trap of the enemy. Choose to surround yourself with "Elishas." Choose to listen to God-led wise counsel. Listen to the wisdom of God-sent counsel. Choose to search and study the Word of God for His answers. Surrender to His solution. Surrender to God and His Way of doing things.

Proverbs 11:14 KJV declares, "Where no counsel is, the people fall: but in the multitude of counsellors there is safety." The Amplified Version expounds on Proverbs 11:14 AMPC in the following manner, "Where no wise guidance is, the people fall, but in the multitude of counselors there is safety."

Surround yourself with wise God-led mentors. Surround your family and your marriage with happy, wise, and God-led couples. Don't contaminate your garden with counselors who are bitter, resentful, and stubborn. Bitter counsel produces bitter fruit. Strengthen your marriage by surrounding yourself with Godly couples who sow Godly advice.

Bitterness has no place in your garden. Resentment has no place in your marriage. Pride destroys families and bitterness corrodes marriages from the inside out. "The way of a fool is right in his own eyes: but he that hearkeneth unto counsel is wise." Proverbs 12:15 KJV.

In 2 Kings 6:9 KJV, Elisha represents good and Godly counsel. Notice the advice that Elisha gives to the king of Israel in 2 Kings 6:9 AMPC, "Beware that you pass not such a place, for the Syrians are coming down there." Elisha declares that the Syrians are coming. Elisha clearly outlines the trap that the enemy was setting up for the king of Israel. Godly counsel identifies traps that you cannot see.

In fact, Godly counselors can warn you and point out dangers that are harmful to the health and welfare of your family and your marriage. Godly counselors can help you navigate through the difficult storms of life. Godly counsel and counselors can help you avoid the "land mines" set by the enemy that was meant for your destruction. Godly counselors are a reflection of

God's Word. Don't listen to the counsel of the ungodly. Submit to the counsel of the Godly.

Psalms 1:1–6 KJV declares, "Blessed is the man that walketh not in the counsel of the ungodly, nor standeth in the way of sinners, nor sitteth in the seat of the scornful. But his delight is in the law of the Lord; and in his law doth he meditate day and night. And he shall be like a tree planted by the rivers of water, that bringeth forth his fruit in his season; his leaf also shall not wither; and whatsoever he doeth shall prosper. The ungodly are not so: but are like the chaff which the wind driveth away. Therefore the ungodly shall not stand in the judgment, nor sinners in the congregation of the righteous. For the Lord knoweth the way of the righteous: but the way of the ungodly shall perish."

## COUPLES' PRAYER

Father God, in the Name of Jesus, we thank You for our marriage. We thank You for Your Word and Your Counsel. Father, we thank You that Your Word leads, guides, and directs our path.

Lord, lead us. Lord, remove the stains of the past. Father, we forgive each other. We forgive those who have sinned against us. We forgive those who have talked about us. We forgive those who have gossiped about us. We forgive those who have conspired against us.

Our hearts are pure and our hands are clean. We wash our hearts in Your Word. We choose to honor You. We choose to submit to Your Counsel. We choose to submit and surrender to Your Word.

In Jesus' Name. Amen.

---

# Day 5

## GOD'S REDIRECTION

*Then the king of Israel sent to the place of which [Elisha] told and warned him; and thus he protected and saved himself there repeatedly.*

2 KINGS 6:10 AMPC

There is a difference between "fear-based" counsel and a God-given warning. Godly counsel gives guidance in an effort to warn or to redirect you in order to protect you. Let's use Elisha's instruction as an example. 2 Kings 6:9 AMPC declares, "Then the man of God sent to the king of Israel, saying, Beware that you pass not such a place, for the Syrians are coming down there." God used Elisha to redirect the path of the king of Israel.

In 2 Kings 6:9 KJV, it appears that the king of Israel was heading down a path that would have collided into the Syrians—"the exalted ones." Remember, according to Strong's Concordance, the Hebrew word for "Syria" is "Aram" (H758), which means, "Exalted."

Notice in 2 Kings 6:9 AMPC, Elisha, God's counsel, explains to the king of Israel, that the "Syrians" were coming. God-led counsel will prevent you from being ambushed. Submit to God-led counsel, and you will not fall victim to the enemy's devices.

Notice the wisdom in Elisha's words in 2 Kings 6:9 KJV, "Beware that thou pass not such a place; for thither the Syrians are come down." Notice, this passage begins with the word "Beware" or "Caution." Elisha warned the king of Israel of what I call a "Caution Zone." Attacks can come from various sources. Sometimes attacks can come from outside of your home, and sometimes they can come from inside the walls of your marriage. Godly counsel will help you navigate around "Caution Zones" outside and within the walls of your marriage.

Every marriage has sensitive subjects and delicate seasons. These topics and areas of discussion are to be handled with wisdom, grace, care, and love. Sometimes, sensitive subjects can be brought up "out of season," causing you to mishandle the heart of your spouse.

Ecclesiastes 3:1 KJV declares, "To every thing there is a season, and a time to every purpose under the heaven:" There is a time and a place for everything. Don't ignore the problem. Don't ignore the hurt. Handle the matter with wisdom. Seek God first before you discuss this "sensitive" topic. Your flesh may want to handle the matter immediately. Your heart may want to discuss it promptly. Choose to surrender your flesh and your heart to God. Go to Him in prayer. Seek God's counsel on the matter. Ask God for wisdom before you go to your spouse. Ask God to soften your heart before you handle the matter.

The Bible declares in 1 Peter 3:7 KJV, "Likewise, ye husbands, dwell with them according to knowledge, giving honour unto the wife, as unto the weaker vessel, and as being heirs together of the grace of life; that your prayers be not hindered." Handle your spouse according to knowledge. In other words, you have intimate knowledge of how to handle your spouse's vulnerable spots. You know your spouse's "weak" areas. You know your spouse's "hot buttons." You know your spouse's "sensitive" areas. Handle your spouse's heart according to your intimate knowledge and intel concerning the situation.

If the sensitive subject is finances, then choose to seek God and ask God for the appropriate and proper time to bring up the matter. If the matter is about sex, romance, and/or intimacy, choose to surrender your heart to God and ask Him for wisdom on how to approach your spouse in a gracious, loving, and heartfelt manner. If the sensitive subject is about a particular family matter, choose to submit to God and ask Him for wisdom on how to lead your heart and handle the matter appropriately.

Choose to approach these "Caution Zones" in a wise, God-led, seasoned, mature, and thoughtful way. Choose to extend grace. Choose to forgive freely. Choose to forgive quickly. Choose to forgive often. Let your words minister grace, peace, and mercy. Sow love. Sow grace. Sow peace. Sow into the ground of your home. Invest in the heart of your marriage.

Let God lead your heart before you respond prematurely out of anger or frustration. Let God soften your heart before you respond out of strife. Let God heal your heart before you respond out of bitterness. Choose to be selfless and let God lead your conversation.

Remember, Elisha's instruction redirected the king of Israel's footsteps in order to avoid a catastrophe. Let God redirect your heart before you lead your family into a chaotic zone. 1 Corinthians 14:33 KJV declares, "For God is not the author of confusion, but of peace." God will not lead you into chaos. Let God's Word lead your house. Let His Word fill your house with His Peace.

Choose to find ways to make peace. Choose to find ways to sow peace. Choose to season your words with His Grace and

Peace. Proverbs 15:1 KJV declares, "A soft answer turneth away wrath: but grievous words stir up anger." Proverbs 15:1 NLT declares, "A gentle answer deflects anger, but harsh words make tempers flare."

Choose to kill pride and submit to humility. Choose to remember daily what the "king of Syria" name means, "Exalted." Exaltation destroys marriages. Don't let anything that's ungodly magnify itself within the walls of your home. "Pride goeth before destruction, and an haughty spirit before a fall." Proverbs 16:18 KJV.

Notice what 2 Kings 6:10 AMPC declares, "Then the king of Israel sent to the place of which [Elisha] told and warned him; and thus he protected and saved himself there repeatedly." When the Godly king, the king of Israel, listened to Godly counsel, Elisha, he and the House of Israel were protected and were repeatedly saved. Choose to crush pride. Instead of wanting to "be right," choose to protect your marriage by consistently listening to wise and Godly counsel. Crucify your flesh daily. Surrender your words to God. Surrender your actions to Christ.

James 1:19 KJV declares, "Wherefore, my beloved brethren, let every man be swift to hear, slow to speak, slow to wrath:" Choose to be swift to hear and slow to speak. Mark 4:23 KJV teaches us, "If any man have ears to hear, let him hear." Choose to hear the heart of your spouse and season your words with grace. "The instruction of the wise is like a life-giving fountain; those who accept it avoid the snares of death." Proverbs 13:14 NLT.

# COUPLES' PRAYER

Father God, in the Name of Jesus, we surrender every aspect of our marriage over to You. Father, redirect our hearts. Lord, lead our language. Father, guide our tongue. Lord, let us be swift to hear, slow to speak, and slow to wrath.

Father, let Your Love guard our words. Lord, let Your Love guide our borders. Father, let Your Love rewrite the pattern of our marriage. Let Your Word be the fingerprint in our family's lives. Lord, soften and lead our hearts forever.

Father, we trust You. Lord, redirect our thoughts and lead us. Father, give us Your framework and strengthen the walls of our marriage. We surrender to You forever.

In Jesus' Name. Amen.

# Day 6

## DEATH AND LIFE

*Death and life are in the power of the tongue:
and they that love it shall eat the fruit thereof.*

PROVERBS 18:21 KJV

Your words have power, and they can establish the course of your marriage. Your words can also derail the destiny of your household. Proverbs 18:21 MSG puts it this way, "Words kill, words give life; they're either poison or fruit—you choose."

Your words can contaminate the garden of your home. Your words can redirect the course of your marriage. Your words can build up, and they also can tear down—it's your choice. Deuteronomy 30:14–16 KJV declares, "But the word is very nigh unto thee, in thy mouth, and in thy heart, that thou mayest do it. See, I have set before thee this day life and good, and death and evil; In that I command thee this day to love the Lord thy God, to walk in his ways, and to keep his commandments and his statutes and his judgments, that thou mayest live and multiply: and the Lord thy God shall bless thee in the land whither thou goest to possess it." Success and defeat are in your mouth. Life and death are in the power of your tongue. Choose your words wisely.

When you choose to contaminate your marriage with negative words, you're choosing to tear down your household. When you choose to throw "emotional daggers" at your spouse—ultimately, you're wounding yourself. Mark 10:8 KJV declares, "And they twain shall be one flesh: so then they are no more twain, but one flesh." So the venom that you spew toward one another ultimately destroys the internal framework of your home.

Ephesians 5:28–29 KJV declares, "So ought men to love their wives as their own bodies. He that loveth his wife loveth himself. For no man ever yet hated his own flesh; but nourisheth and cherisheth it, even as the Lord the church:" Husbands, nourish your wife with your words. Wives, nourish your husband with your words. Love your spouse as your own body. You both are one flesh. Think about this scripture the next time you decide to throw that venomous "word dagger" toward one another.

James 1:19 KJV declares, "Wherefore, my beloved brethren, let every man be swift to hear, slow to speak, slow to wrath:" Choose to hear her. Choose to hear him. Choose to hear what the Word has to say before you give your opinion. Don't allow your emotions to rule your conversation. Choose to surrender your heart to God and season your words with His Grace. Ephesians 4:29 KJV declares, "Let no corrupt communication proceed out of your mouth, but that which is good to the use of edifying, that it may minister grace unto the hearers."

Notice what James 3:4–5 KJV declares, "Behold also the ships, which though they be so great, and are driven of fierce winds, yet are they turned about with a very small helm, whithersoever the governor listeth. Even so the tongue is a little member, and boasteth great things. Behold, how great a matter a little fire kindleth!" Your words matter. Like the helm of a ship, your words direct the course of your life, family, destiny, and marriage.

Words carry weight. Words, when used properly, are God's tool to display man's authority in the Earth. God gave man the gift of language in order to build, identify, construct, and to set in order. Genesis 2:18–24 KJV declares, "And the Lord God said, It is not good that the man should be alone; I will make him an help meet for him. And out of the ground the Lord God formed every beast of the field, and every fowl of the air; and brought them unto Adam to see what he would call them: and whatsoever Adam called every living creature, that was the name thereof. And Adam gave names to all cattle, and to the fowl of the air, and to every beast of the field; but for Adam there was not found an help meet for him. And the Lord God caused a deep sleep to fall upon Adam, and he slept: and he took one of his ribs, and closed up the flesh instead thereof; And the rib, which the Lord God had taken from man, made he a woman, and brought her unto the man. And Adam said, This is now bone of my bones, and flesh of my flesh: she shall be called Woman, because she was taken out of Man. Therefore shall a man leave his father and his mother, and shall cleave unto his wife: and they shall be one flesh."

God gave Adam authority to name every beast of the field, the fowl of the air, and every living thing. God presented His creation to Adam, and whatever Adam named it—that was the name. Names and words carry weight. Words carry authority. Words identify purpose.

When words are used out of context, or when they are perverted—they have the opposite effect. Contaminated words contaminate hearts. Perverse words corrupt marriages. Bitter words destroy generations. You can speak blessings, or you can speak curses over your spouse, over your family, and over your children—you choose.

Jesus states in John 6:63 KJV, "It is the spirit that quickeneth; the flesh profiteth nothing: the words that I speak unto you, they are spirit, and they are life." God's Word is life. Speak life over your children. Speak life over your marriage. Speak life over your spouse. Speak life over your family. Speak peace. Speak success. Sow seeds of life into the heart of your home and watch God rewrite the legacy of your marriage, life, and family. Speak life.

What seeds are you sowing? What roots are embedded in the ground of your marriage? Are they seeds of bitterness? Are they seeds of confusion? Are they seeds of chaos? Are they seeds of fear? Are they seeds of discord? Or, are they seeds of life? Seeds of success? Seeds of peace? Seeds of grace? Choose to sow the Word of God. Sow life into your spouse. Sow life into your family. Sow life into your marriage.

"For the Word that God speaks is alive and full of power [making it active, operative, energizing, and effective]; it is sharper than any two-edged sword, penetrating to the dividing line of the breath of life (soul) and [the immortal] spirit, and of joints and marrow [of the deepest parts of our nature], exposing and sifting and analyzing and judging the very thoughts and purposes of the heart." Hebrews 4:12 AMPC. Remember to choose your words wisely. Let God lead the language of your home.

Over time, seeds have the ability to grow roots. Eventually, these roots develop a system within the soil of your heart. What "root system" are you creating within the foundation of your marriage? Dig deep into the soil of your home and sow life continually.

## COUPLES' PRAYER

Father God, in the Name of Jesus, we thank You for our marriage. Father, we thank You for leading and guiding our home. Father, we thank You for leading and guiding our footsteps. Father, we ask that You lead our words. Lord, lead our lips to reflect Your Heart and Character.

Father, lead this house. We choose to speak success in the midst of defeat. We choose to speak life in the midst of death and destruction. We choose to meditate on Your Word and confess it day and night.

Lord, Your Word carries weight in our lives. Lord, we value Your Word over man's opinion. Father, Your Word reigns supreme. Lord, our house chooses to worship You forever.

In Jesus' Mighty Name. Amen.

# Day 7

# A GOOD NAME

*A good name is rather to be chosen than great riches, and loving favour rather than silver and gold.*

PROVERBS 22:1 KJV

Let God rewrite your character. Let God rewrite your reputation. Let God rewrite your family's name. Let God free you from the bondage of the past. Choose to keep a good name and let God rewrite your destiny. Let God transform the heart of your marriage. His Word will set you free. When you surrender to God, your life is transformed. When you surrender to God, your name is transformed. When you are in Christ, everything attached to you is renewed. Let God renew your marriage. Let God renew your heart. Let God refresh and restore your soul through your obedience and submission to Him.

When you submit to God, He will lead and soften the ground of your heart. When you surrender to Him, He will renew your mind. When you surrender to Him, He will transform you from the inside out. When you surrender to Christ, He will transform your name, reputation, and character. In fact, according to 2 Corinthians 5:17 KJV, when you are in Christ, you are a whole new creature: "Therefore if any man be in Christ, he is a new creature: old things are passed away; behold, all things are become new."

Saul, a murderer and a Pharisee, was turned into Paul—an Apostle to the Gentiles. Jacob, a deceiving, opportunistic trickster, was turned into Israel—a man after God's Heart. Abram, a man without an heir, was turned into Abraham—the father of many.

Names have meaning. God is constantly in the business of rewriting names, legacies, and lineages. When God changes your name, He changes the spiritual weight attached to it. When God changed someone's name in the Bible, it elevated their reputation naturally and increased their weight spiritually.

Because of Abram's obedience, faith, and faithfulness—his name was changed into Abraham "The Father of Many." Abraham's spiritual weight and natural authority changed because he obeyed God. This man, who had no heir, simply obeyed God and became—"The Father of Many." He obeyed God, stepped out on faith, and he was able to pronounce "The Blessing" over his God-given seed. Names and words have power and authority.

Even Jesus had a good reputation with God and man. Luke 2:52 NLT declares, "Jesus grew in wisdom and in stature and in favor with God and all the people." Proverbs 22:1 AMPC declares, "A GOOD name is rather to be chosen than great riches, and loving favor rather than silver and gold."

A good name carries more weight and spiritual authority than silver and gold. Psalms 24:3-4 KJV declares, "Who shall ascend into the hill of the Lord? or who shall stand in his holy place? He that hath clean hands, and a pure heart; who hath not lifted up his soul unto vanity, nor sworn deceitfully."

Promotion comes from God. Ascension is linked to clean hands and a pure heart; in other words, choose to keep a good reputation, and clean spiritual character—don't pervert the gift for gold. Proverbs 22:1 NLT declares, "Choose a good reputation over great riches; being held in high esteem is better than silver or gold."

When you are in Christ, your name carries weight on Earth and in Heaven. Look at this spiritual conversation between God and Satan concerning the spiritual integrity and moral character of Job. "One day the members of the heavenly court came to present themselves before the Lord, and the accuser, Satan, came with them. "Where have you come from?" the Lord asked Satan. Satan answered the Lord, "I have been patrolling the earth, watching everything that's going on." Then the Lord asked Satan, "Have you considered my servant Job? He is the finest man in all the earth. He is blameless—a man of complete integrity. He fears God and stays away from evil." Job 1:6–8 NLT.

God told Satan, "Have you considered my servant Job? He is the finest man in all the earth. He is blameless—a man of complete integrity. He fears God and stays away from evil." Job's moral character and spiritual integrity was known in Heaven and on Earth. Your character matters. Spiritual integrity matters. Obedience matters. Choose to submit to God and allow God to lead your heart and character. Allow God to lead your family's course.

God recommended Job. Can God recommend you? What does Heaven say about you? What does God declare about you? Sit still before Him and let God speak over you. Let God sing over you. Let His Word breathe into every part of your heart. Let His Word breathe over and into every aspect of your marriage.

2 Corinthians 5:17 KJV declares, "Therefore if any man be in Christ, he is a new creature: old things are passed away; behold, all things are become new." When you are in Christ, every old thing about your life transforms. Romans 12:2 KJV declares, "And be not conformed to this world: but be ye transformed by the renewing of your mind, that ye may prove what is that good, and acceptable, and perfect, will of God."

When you are in Christ, your old man passes away. When you submit your life to God, He will give you a fresh start. When you submit your heart to God, He will give you a new beginning. But it's up to you to walk in everything that He has for you. Choose to obey God and walk free in Him. Let the past go, and walk new in Christ. "Therefore if any person is [ingrafted] in Christ (the Messiah) he is a new creation (a new creature altogether); the old [previous moral and spiritual condition] has passed away. Behold, the fresh and new has come!" 2 Corinthians 5:17 AMPC.

When you are engrafted in Christ, you are a new creature all together. The old previous moral and spiritual condition has passed away—and behold all things have become new. Don't pattern your ways, thoughts, habits, and actions after the old man—walk new in Christ. Let the fresh come in. Let the newness of Christ fill your home, heart, and your marriage. Don't pick up the old way of doing things—choose to pick up Christ's Way of doing things. His Way is better.

## COUPLES' PRAYER

Father God, in the Name of Jesus, we thank You for leading our home. Father, we thank You for softening the ground of our heart. Father, we thank You for softening the heart of our marriage.

Father, we surrender to Your Will. Lord, we surrender to Your Way. Father, teach us to follow You. Lord, let the heart of our marriage reflect Your Heart.

Father, let our character, in private and in public, reflect Your Character. Lord, we choose to trust You now and forever.

In Jesus' Name. Amen.

# Day 8

## FOUL COMMUNICATION CORRUPTS MARRIAGES

*Let no corrupt communication proceed out of your mouth, but that which is good to the use of edifying, that it may minister grace unto the hearers.*

EPHESIANS 4:29 KJV

Let no corrupt communication come from your mouth. Choose your words wisely. Proverbs 18:21 KJV declares, "Death and life are in the power of the tongue: and they that love it shall eat the fruit thereof." Your words have power. Your words have authority. Your words carry weight. Your words have the ability to steer the course of your marriage. Your words can lead and direct the course of your life and marriage.

When storms arise, choose to steer your house with the Word of God. Proverbs 18:21 NLT declares, "The tongue can bring death or life; those who love to talk will reap the consequences." Choose to speak God's Word. Choose to say what God says about your marriage. Choose to say what God says about your family. Choose to say what God says about your house. Let His Word steer your course.

When storms arise, you can either argue and cause your home to shipwreck—or you can let God lead your words and redirect the course of your house. The choice is up to you. Let God lead your language.

Ephesians 4:29 AMPC declares, "Let no foul or polluting language, nor evil word nor unwholesome or worthless talk [ever] come out of your mouth, but only such [speech] as is good and beneficial to the spiritual progress of others, as is fitting to the need and the occasion, that it may be a blessing and give grace (God's favor) to those who hear it." Don't pollute the ground of your marriage with foul and corrupt communication.

Pattern your character, speech, and conduct after Christ. Pattern your language after Christ. Pattern your actions after Christ. Don't pollute the ground of your marriage through reckless communication and contaminated words of strife. Contaminated seeds will produce a contaminated harvest.

Think about it, if you continue to live on the shame, guilt, pain, and mistakes of the past, you'll stay stuck in the moment of the offense. Choose to forgive and wash the slate of your marriage clean. Whenever you recklessly bring up the past, you're sowing seeds of discord. Choose to let God heal your heart. Let God heal every aspect of your marriage. Let God lead and heal your heart and language. Choose your words wisely.

There are countless examples throughout the Bible, where God shows us how to handle the pain, mistrust, shame, and offense of the past. Choose to let the Word of God lead you through the pain of the past. Let His Word free your soul. Let His Word free you completely. Let His Word lead the language framework of your marriage. Don't be led by reckless emotions. Surrender to God. Let God lead and heal your emotions. Let

God heal your heart. Broken hearts hurt people. Don't let the pain of the past contaminate the ground of your marriage.

Ezekiel 36:26 NLT declares, "And I will give you a new heart, and I will put a new spirit in you. I will take out your stony, stubborn heart and give you a tender, responsive heart." Let God take out your stony heart. Let God give you a new heart. Let God take out the bitterness of the past. Let His Word heal you. Let His Word restore you. Let His Word set you free.

Give your old heart over to God and let Him replace it with a new, tender, and responsive heart. Choose to forgive freely, frequently, and often. Don't let the contamination of the past harden the heart of your marriage. Don't let the poison of the past linger in the soil of your heart. Let God conduct heart surgery on every aspect of your heart. Let God conduct heart surgery on your marriage. Let His Word soften your heart.

Let His Word heal you. Let the regret of the past go. Let the tears of the past go. Let the hurt of the past go. Let the pain of the past go. Choose to let the shame and the deep-seated contamination of the past go. Let God change your language toward your spouse. Let God heal and lead your language toward your family.

Let God use your words to minister toward one another. Let God use your words to lead and build up your family. Let God use your words to build up your marriage. Let God use your words to build up your spouse. Let your words be filled with love, mercy, peace, and grace.

Let your legacy be remembered as the one who handles the heart of others in honor, love, and respect. Choose to establish the pattern of love, mercy, grace, and forgiveness within the walls of your marriage. Choose to establish the pattern of peace within the borders of your family.

Choose to forgive freely. Forgiveness is a weapon. When you forgive, you set your heart free. Forgive those who have wronged you. Forgive those who have offended you. Forgive freely, frequently, and often.

A matured heart freely forgives. A healed heart forgives. Learn to speak the language of forgiveness. When you've been hurt, you have a choice to either stay in the emotional prison of the transgression—or you can be set free by forgiving those who have hurt you. Learn to forgive.

Matthew 18:21–22 MSG declares, "At that point Peter got up the nerve to ask, "Master, how many times do I forgive a brother or sister who hurts me? Seven?" Jesus replied, "Seven! Hardly. Try seventy times seven." Pattern your house after the forgiveness framework that Christ outlined in Matthew 18:21–22. Choose to forgive freely, frequently, and often. Set your heart free and let the pain of the past go.

## COUPLES' PRAYER

Father God, in the Name of Jesus, thank You for leading our marriage. Lord, we choose to surrender every aspect of our language over to You.

Lord, cleanse the heart of our marriage. Father, let the words that proceed out of our mouth please You. We choose to let our words minister grace, peace, and love.

Father, we choose to forgive one another. We choose to let the bondage of the past go. We choose to let the pain of the past go. We choose to forgive and let the freedom of Christ reign within the borders of our house.

Lord, we honor You. We love You. We choose to exalt You now and forever.

In Jesus' Name. Amen.

# Day 9

# A CARNAL MARRIAGE

*Because the carnal mind is enmity against God: for it is not subject to the law of God, neither indeed can be.*

ROMANS 8:7 KJV

An emotionally reckless marriage is hostile against God. A marriage filled with bitterness, strife, and discord is enmity against God. Romans 8:7 AMPC declares, "[That is] because the mind of the flesh [with its carnal thoughts and purposes] is hostile to God, for it does not submit itself to God's Law; indeed it cannot."

A hostile marriage does not have peace within its borders. In fact, a divided house is unstable and wars against God and against one another. Proverbs 25:24 KJV declares, "It is better to dwell in the corner of the housetop, than with a brawling woman and in a wide house." The Amplified Version expounds upon Proverbs 25:24 this way, "It is better to dwell in the corner of the housetop than to share a house with a disagreeing, quarrelsome, and scolding woman."

Choose to have peace within the borders of your marriage. Choose to pattern your actions after Christ. A hostile marriage is a divided house. Let God lead your peace within the borders of your marriage. Handle your spouse with wisdom. Handle your spouse with love. Handle your spouse with grace.

Men, let God lead your heart as you lead your family. Husbands, let God lead your words as you lead your wife. Let God give you the words to say. Let God give you the words to sow into her. Let God give you the words to invest into her. Spend time in the Word. As a family, spend time together in the Word.

Matthew 12:25 KJV declares, "And Jesus knew their thoughts, and said unto them, Every kingdom divided against itself is brought to desolation; and every city or house divided against itself shall not stand:" Empires fall when a family is divided. Families fall when a house is divided. Kingdoms fall when a marriage is divided. Let God lead and transform your heart. Let God lead and transform your house.

Men, God has given you your family as a gift to lead and to steward. As the head of the home, we are to lead and to steward the gift that God has given us by obeying His Voice and submitting to God's Counsel.

A submitted heart will surrender to God's Way of doing things. Men, let God lead your heart and your house, and you will never shipwreck. "Husbands, love your wives, even as Christ also loved the church, and gave himself for it;" Ephesians 5:25 KJV.

A marriage that is selfless will succeed and thrive. Selflessly sow into one another. Selflessly build up one another. Selflessly speak life into one another. Selflessly invest in one another. Selflessly learn about one another. Selflessly give. Selflessly pour into one another. A house that's selfless will establish a "Love Blueprint" for generations to follow.

Consider your spouse before you consider yourself. Pray for your spouse before you selfishly think about yourself. Selflessly pray for doors of opportunity and platforms to open for your spouse. Speak life over your spouse at home, in private, and in public. Selflessly lift up the heart of your spouse. A selfless marriage chooses to focus on and is patterned after Christ.

Joshua 1:8 NLT declares, "Study this Book of Instruction continually. Meditate on it day and night so you will be sure to obey everything written in it. Only then will you prosper and succeed in all you do." Pattern your marriage after the Word of God—and you will have good success.

Let His Word selflessly feed the heart of your marriage. Let His Word nourish your heart. Let His Word feed your family. Matthew 4:4 KJV declares, "But he answered and said, It is written, Man shall not live by bread alone, but by every word that proceedeth out of the mouth of God." Feed your family God's Word daily. Study His Word and let His Word guide your heart and lead the affairs of your family.

Jeremiah 3:15 KJV declares, "And I will give you pastors according to mine heart, which shall feed you with knowledge and understanding." Jeremiah 3:15 AMPC declares, "And I will give you [spiritual] shepherds after My own heart [in the final time], who will feed you with knowledge and understanding and judgment." Let God lead your family and plant you under a pastor after His Own Heart. Let God minister to you through your pastor. A pastor, or a spiritual shepherd, is a gift from God who is trained, called, anointed, and positioned by God to watch over and to steward your soul.

Psalms 1:1–2 KJV declares, "Blessed is the man that walketh not in the counsel of the ungodly, nor standeth in the way of sinners, nor sitteth in the seat of the scornful. But his delight is in the law of the Lord; and in his law doth he meditate day and night." Blessed are those who choose to plant themselves in

God's Word. Blessed are those who obey God's Word. Choose to meditate on His Word day and night. His Counsel is His Word. Submit to God's Counsel. Submit to His Word.

Your pastor is a part of your Godly counsel. God plants Pastors in the earth to feed and to oversee His sheep; And as God's sheep, He will not leave your family in the wilderness to die. God wants your marriage to flourish. God wants your family to thrive. God wants you planted. God wants every part of your life and your marriage to flourish.

3 John 1:2 KJV declares, "Beloved, I wish above all things that thou mayest prosper and be in health, even as thy soul prospereth." God wants every aspect of your life, heart, marriage, ministry, business, and purpose to succeed. God wants you to prosper. The Amplified Version puts 3 John 1:2 this way, "Beloved, I pray that you may prosper in every way and [that your body] may keep well, even as [I know] your soul keeps well and prospers."

God wants you to prosper in every way. So choose to surrender the old things over to Him. Choose to surrender the past over to Him. Surrender the hidden things over to Him. A carnal marriage holds on to the dead things of the past. Choose to let go of the old and fill your life, marriage, and ministry with the new things of Christ. Your family is your ministry. Your marriage is your ministry. Let God lead and transform your destiny. Surrender your marriage to Christ.

## COUPLES' PRAYER

Father God, in the Name of Jesus, we choose to submit to You. Lord, we choose to submit to one another. Lord, we choose to let go of the old things, and we choose to focus on You.

Lord, lead our hearts. Father, we will forever surrender to Your Voice. Lord, heal every aspect of our family. Father, strengthen every aspect of our marriage.

Lord, according to 1 Peter 5:7 KJV, we cast every care, worry, and concern over to You. Father, fear will not rule the heart of our marriage. We choose to have a heart that reflects You. Father, we surrender to You.

In Jesus' Name. Amen.

## Day 10

## OLD WINE

*And he spake also a parable unto them; No man putteth a piece of a new garment upon an old; if otherwise, then both the new maketh a rent, and the piece that was taken out of the new agreeth not with the old. And no man putteth new wine into old bottles; else the new wine will burst the bottles, and be spilled, and the bottles shall perish. But new wine must be put into new bottles; and both are preserved. No man also having drunk old wine straightway desireth new: for he saith, The old is better.*

LUKE 5:36-39 KJV

Desire God's Way of doing things. Choose to desire Him. Crave Him. Be led by God in every area of your life. Luke 5:36 KJV declares, "No man putteth a piece of a new garment upon an old; if otherwise, then both the new maketh a rent, and the piece that was taken out of the new agreeth not with the old." Luke 5:36 APMC declares, "No one puts a patch from a new garment on an old garment; if he does, he will both tear the new one, and the patch from the new [one] will not match the old [garment]."

When God gives you new instruction about your life, marriage, ministry, business, purpose, or family choose to submit to the new garment. Choose to submit to His Way. Choose to submit to the new Way of doing things. The "new" patch of instruction will not agree with the old framework. Let the old things go. Let the old patch go. Let the old way of doing things die. Walk forward in new life. Walk forward in unity. Walk forward in everything that God has for you.

Choose to receive the new wine. Receive God's new and fresh Way of doing things. Forgive your spouse. Forgive yourself. Forgive your enemies. Forgive your family members. Forgive everyone who has come up against you and choose to receive the new garment. Receive God's pattern. Receive God's instruction. Receive God's blueprint.

Maybe, you're trying to put old things back into your marriage. Maybe you're trying to put old habits back into your marriage. Maybe, you're trying to put old people back into your marriage. Let the past go and cling to God. Let the dead things die and let the dead bury the dead. Let the old things of the past die in the past.

Galatians 5:1 KJV declares, "Stand fast therefore in the liberty wherewith Christ hath made us free, and be not entangled again with the yoke of bondage." Do not be entangled by the bondage of the past. Let the old man go. Let the old man wither and die. Let the old patterns and old habits wither and die. Don't touch the old things—embrace the new Way of doing things.

Remember Lot's wife? She held on to the past—she looked back. According to Genesis 19:24-26 KJV, "Then the Lord rained upon Sodom and upon Gomorrah brimstone and fire from the Lord out of heaven; And he overthrew those cities, and all the plain, and all the inhabitants of the cities, and that which grew upon the ground. But his wife looked back from behind him, and she became a pillar of salt." Don't look back. Don't desire the things of the old. Don't crave the things of the old, or else, you'll stay stuck in the past and grow stagnant.

Don't let your marriage grow stagnant by craving the things of the past. Let the old appetites go. Let the old appetites die. Let the old desires go. Surrender your heart and life to Christ. Choose to crave Christ.

Luke 5:37 KJV declares, "And no man putteth new wine into old bottles; else the new wine will burst the bottles, and be spilled, and the bottles shall perish." Luke 5:37 AMPC declares, "And no one pours new wine into old wineskins; if he does, the fresh wine will burst the skins and it will be spilled and the skins will be ruined (destroyed)." When you crave the things of the past, not only will your marriage stay stuck but it will collapse and burst. You can't mix the old with the new.

Let God transform the heart of your marriage. Let God transform the wineskin of your marriage. Let God cover you. Let God heal you. Let God lead you. A selfish and carnal marriage chooses to do things their way. It is difficult for a selfish and carnal marriage to develop and grow. In fact, a selfish heart is stubborn and cannot surrender to God's Way of doing things. Surrender your heart and your marriage completely to God.

Luke 5:38 KJV declares, "But new wine must be put into new bottles; and both are preserved." Choose to completely crave Christ. Crave the new things. Let God strengthen the walls of your heart. Let God rebuild the walls of your marriage.

Colossians 3:10 KJV declares, "And have put on the new man, which is renewed in knowledge after the image of him that created him:" Put on the new man. Put on the ways of Christ. Let God renew you. Let God renew your heart. Let God renew your marriage. Let God renew every part of your life. Wash your language through His Word. Let His Word lead every aspect of your marriage.

Philippians 2:5 KJV declares, "Let this mind be in you, which was also in Christ Jesus:" According to Strong's Concordance, the Greek word for "Mind" is "phroneō" (G5426), which means "To have understanding, to be wise, to feel, to think, to have an opinion of one's self, think of one's self, to be modest, not let one's opinion (though just) of himself exceed the bounds of modesty, to think or judge what one's opinion is, to be of the same mind i.e. agreed together, cherish the same views, be harmonious, to direct one's mind to a thing, to seek, to strive for, to seek one's interest or advantage, to be of one's party, side with him (in public affairs)." Let the framework of your marriage surrender to Christ. Let your heart side with Christ. Let the "mind" of your marriage agree with the Heart of Christ. Choose to agree with His Word. Choose to agree and walk together in love.

## A HUSBAND'S PRAYER

Father God, in the Name of Jesus, I thank You for my wife. Father, I thank You for Your daughter. Lord, I thank You that she is full of wisdom, favor, character, grace, love, and insight. Lord, I thank You that her heart reflects You. Father, I thank You that her heart reflects Your Character.

Lord, I thank You for my family. Father, I declare that we are a house that represents You. Father, I declare, in the Name of Jesus, that my house reflects Your Heart and we choose to submit to You.

Father, I declare, that my house is full of peace, wisdom, insight, and nations shall call us blessed. Lord, we surrender our hearts to You now and forever.

In Jesus' Name. Amen.

## A WIFE'S PRAYER

Father God, in the Name of Jesus, I thank You for my husband. Father, I thank You for Your son. Lord, I thank You that he is full of wisdom, character, and insight. Father, I thank You that his heart reflects Your Character.

Lord, I thank You for my family. Father, I declare that we are a house that represents You. Father, I declare, in the Name of Jesus, that our house reflects Your Heart and we submit to You.

Father, I declare, that our house is full of peace, wisdom, insight, and nations shall call us blessed. Lord, we surrender our hearts to You. Lord, lead us.

In Jesus' Name. Amen.

## Day 11

# WALK TOGETHER

*Can two walk together, except they be agreed?*

AMOS 3:3 KJV

Can two walk together unless they agree? Can two live together unless they agree? Can two do life together unless they agree? Proverbs 25:24 KJV declares, "It is better to dwell in the corner of the housetop, than with a brawling woman and in a wide house." According to Proverbs 25:24 AMPC, "It is better to dwell in the corner of the housetop than to share a house with a disagreeing, quarrelsome, and scolding woman."

Choose to let peace flourish within the borders of your home. Fight for peace. Fight for one another and not against each other. "Let no corrupt communication proceed out of your mouth, but that which is good to the use of edifying, that it may minister grace unto the hearers." Ephesians 4:29 KJV. Let your words minister to one another. Let your deeds and actions build up one another. Let the language of your home strengthen one another. Redirect your energy to combat against the enemy. Your spouse is not your enemy.

Luke 22:31–32 KJV declares, "And the Lord said, Simon, Simon, behold, Satan hath desired to have you, that he may sift you as wheat: But I have prayed for thee, that thy faith fail not: and when thou art converted, strengthen thy brethren." Satan desires to sift your marriage and family as wheat. Choose to pray for your family. Choose to protect your home by guarding and by choosing your words wisely. Mark 3:25 AMPC declares, "And if a house be divided against itself, that house cannot stand."

Forgive one another and leave the past behind. Forgive one another and leave the offense behind. Luke 22:32 KJV declares, "But I have prayed for thee, that thy faith fail not: and when thou art converted, strengthen thy brethren." Pray for one another. Pray for your house. Pray for the success of your family. Pray for the direction of your family. Choose to pray instead of choosing to argue. Choose to invest in the infrastructure of your marriage.

Let the foundation of your marriage be strengthened by the Word of God. In fact, Ephesians 2:16–22 KJV declares, "And that he might reconcile both unto God in one body by the cross, having slain the enmity thereby: And came and preached peace to you which were afar off, and to them that were nigh. For through him we both have access by one Spirit unto the Father. Now therefore ye are no more strangers and foreigners, but fellowcitizens with the saints, and of the household of God; And are built upon the foundation of the apostles and prophets, Jesus Christ himself being the chief corner stone; In whom all the building fitly framed together groweth unto an holy temple in the Lord: In whom ye also are builded together for an habitation of God through the Spirit."

Let Christ, the Chief Cornerstone, establish your marriage. Let His Word fitly frame every aspect of your home. Build your life on His Word. Let Christ fitly frame every private and hidden part of your heart and marriage upon His Word. Let His Word fitly frame and establish every aspect of your family. Choose to surrender to Him. Let Christ be the Chief Cornerstone of your family. Seek His Peace. Seek His Love. Seek Christ.

Proverbs 2:6 AMPC declares, "For the Lord gives skillful and godly Wisdom; from His mouth come knowledge and understanding." James 1:5 AMPC declares, "If any of you is deficient in wisdom, let him ask of the giving God [Who gives] to everyone liberally and ungrudgingly, without reproaching or faultfinding, and it will be given him." God gives wisdom liberally.

Ask God for wisdom. Ask God for wisdom on how to handle your spouse. Ask God for wisdom on how to handle the heart of your marriage. Ask God to lead your words. Seek wisdom before you respond. Pray together before you speak. Ask God for instruction before you respond. Let God lead your heart. Let God lead your emotions. Amos 3:3 NLT declares, "Can two people walk together without agreeing on the direction?" Let His Word direct the footsteps of your house.

Try this Bible-based exercise the next time a discussion tries to divide you and your spouse: Amos 3:3 AMPC declares, "Do two walk together except they make an appointment and have agreed?" Make an appointment! Before you respond abruptly, before you get into a heated debate—place the subject on the table, pause, reflect, and set an appointment to discuss the matter at an agreed-upon later time.

Proverbs 3:13 KJV declares, "Happy is the man that findeth wisdom, and the man that getteth understanding." In your alone time, pray, and ask God for wisdom on how to handle the heart of your spouse. Pray and ask God how to handle the sensitive matter. Pray and ask God for the grace to handle the heart of your marriage. Ask God for peace and let His Peace lead the framework and fabric of the discussion. Ask God for peace and let His Peace lead the framework and fabric of your home. Pray for one another continually.

## COUPLES' PRAYER

Father God, in the Name of Jesus, I thank You for my spouse. Father, we surrender to You. Father, we surrender every aspect of our hearts over to You. Father, we surrender every aspect of our conversation over to You.

Father, we surrender our marriage over to You. Lord, wash the heart of our marriage in the Blood of Your Son, Jesus Christ. Lord, lead our path and rewrite our language. Lord, order our steps. Father, we forgive each other freely.

Lord, we trust You to lead our thoughts and actions. Father, we trust You to handle our hearts with grace and wisdom. Lord, we trust You to lead our family. Father, we repent and turn to You now and forever.

In Jesus' Name. Amen.

## Day 12

## A NEW START

*Behold, I am doing a new thing! Now it springs forth; do you not perceive and know it and will you not give heed to it? I will even make a way in the wilderness and rivers in the desert.*

ISAIAH 43:19 AMPC

Let God do a new thing within the walls of your marriage. Let the old things go. Let the things of the past go and let God do a brand-new thing in every area of your heart and marriage. Choose not to hold on to the weight, guilt, shame, and defeat of the past. Let the chains of the past go. Let the bondage of the old go.

Isaiah 43:19 AMPC declares, "Behold, I am doing a new thing! Now it springs forth; do you not perceive and know it and will you not give heed to it? I will even make a way in the wilderness and rivers in the desert." Let God break through every area of your marriage. Let His Word spring forth in every part of your heart. Let the old habits, old patterns, and old way of thinking go. Let God transform your heart. Let God transform your marriage.

Romans 12:2 KJV declares, "And be not conformed to this world: but be ye transformed by the renewing of your mind, that ye may prove what is that good, and acceptable, and perfect, will of God." The Amplified Version expounds on Romans 12:2 AMPC in the following manner, "Do not be conformed to this world (this age), [fashioned after and adapted to its external, superficial customs], but be transformed (changed) by the [entire] renewal of your mind [by its new ideals and its new attitude], so that you may prove [for yourselves] what is the good and acceptable and perfect will of God, even the thing which is good and acceptable and perfect [in His sight for you]."

Let God shift your mindset about your marriage. Let God shift your mindset about how you handle the heart of your spouse. Let God shift your mindset about the framework of your family. Let God renew and transform you completely.

I pray, that as you read this message, that God shifts your mind and heals parts of your marriage that you didn't know needed to be healed. I pray that God heals your heart. I pray that you let the former things, the former customs, the former attitudes about your marriage die. Leave the past behind you and let God reorder your steps.

I pray that God transforms the vocabulary of your marriage. I pray that God softens your heart. I pray that God leads your words within the walls of your marriage. I pray that you and your spouse have a desire to please Him. I pray that God turns your heart to Him.

Proverbs 21:1 KJV declares, "The king's heart is in the hand of the Lord, as the rivers of water: he turneth it whithersoever he will." God can turn the heart of your marriage if you surrender it to Him. Let God heal your heart. Let God transform your marriage. Let God make you whole.

Proverbs 26:11 KJV declares, "As a dog returneth to his vomit, so a fool returneth to his folly." Don't turn back to the foolishness of the past. Don't turn back to the vomit of the past. Let God heal your language. Let God heal you from the emotional daggers and reckless wounds of the past. Let His Love set you free. Love heals. Love restores. Love will set your heart free.

Isaiah 10:27 KJV declares, "And it shall come to pass in that day, that his burden shall be taken away from off thy shoulder, and his yoke from off thy neck, and the yoke shall be destroyed because of the anointing." Love breaks yokes. Love breaks cycles. Love breaks stagnation. Let love set you free. Let God free your heart from the guilt, shame, and defeat of the past. Let God remove the wounds of the past.

Let the Love of God break every yoke that's tied to your marriage. In agricultural days, a yoke was a type of harness that was bound to the necks of farming animals that were used to plow and to till the farmer's land. Oftentimes, the farmer (or the master) would yoke together animals as an attempt to tame, guide, or control the team of oxen.

Just as the master farmer used yokes to tame oxen in order to plow the field, the enemy uses "yoking" tactics in the same way. Satan likes to "yoke" you to sin. Satan likes to keep you bound. Satan likes to keep your heart bound to the offense of the past. Satan likes to yoke you to the bondage of the past.

Satan likes to yoke you to familiar and oppressive spirits as a means to control you and to lure you away from your purpose. Galatians 5:1 KJV declares, "Stand fast therefore in the liberty wherewith Christ hath made us free, and be not entangled again with the yoke of bondage." Be not entangled in the bondage of the past.

Matthew 11:28–30 KJV declares, "Come unto me, all ye that labour and are heavy laden, and I will give you rest. Take my yoke upon you, and learn of me; for I am meek and lowly in heart: and ye shall find rest unto your souls. For my yoke is easy, and my burden is light."

Surrender your marriage to God. Give your heart to God; His yoke is easy, and His burden is light. His Way is easy, and His burden is light. Let God lift every burden from off of your marriage. Let God lift every weight from off of your marriage. Let God break every yoke from off of your life. Let God remove the old things. Let the former things go. Let God do a new thing.

## COUPLES' PRAYER

Father God, in the Name of Jesus, we surrender every part of our marriage over to You. Lord, we surrender our hearts over to You. Father, we surrender our family over to You.

Lord, we let go of the bondage of the past. Father, we set our hearts toward You. Lord, heal our hearts. Lord, strengthen our marriage. Father, keep, guard, and protect our marriage from every snare and attack of the enemy.

Lord, let Your Blood cover every aspect of our hearts. Lord, our family honors You, and we submit our ways to You—forever.

In Jesus' Name. Amen.

# Day 13

## WHAT'S DONE IN THE DARK

*For it is a shame even to speak of those things which are done of them in secret.*

EPHESIANS 5:12 KJV

Let God expose the hidden things. Genesis 3:8–11 KJV declares, "And they heard the voice of the Lord God walking in the garden in the cool of the day: and Adam and his wife hid themselves from the presence of the Lord God amongst the trees of the garden. And the Lord God called unto Adam, and said unto him, Where art thou? And he said, I heard thy voice in the garden, and I was afraid, because I was naked; and I hid myself. And he said, Who told thee that thou wast naked? Hast thou eaten of the tree, whereof I commanded thee that thou shouldest not eat?"

Have you eaten from a tree that God has told you not to touch? Have you touched something that God has told you not to touch? Disobedience in private will produce guilt and shame. You can't hide from God. According to Genesis 2:17 KJV, God told Adam not to eat of the tree of the knowledge of good and evil. "But of the tree of the knowledge of good and evil, thou shalt not eat of it: for in the day that thou eatest thereof thou shalt surely die." What you choose to eat in private has generational consequence. Your obedience or disobedience today will impact generations to come.

Disobedience produces cycles. In fact, disobedience causes you to wither. Maybe your marriage is in a withering wilderness cycle because of your private disobedience. Romans 6:23 KJV declares, "For the wages of sin is death; but the gift of God is eternal life through Jesus Christ our Lord." The payment of sin is death. What you choose to do in secret has a lasting generational impact.

Corrupt hearts ruin marriages. Corrupt bed chambers destroy marriages from the inside out. Hebrews 13:4 KJV declares, "Marriage is honourable in all, and the bed undefiled: but whoremongers and adulterers God will judge." Don't let your marriage die because of something that you ate in private. Choose to turn to God who can transform your appetite. Choose to turn to God who can renew your mind and attitude toward the covenant of your marriage.

Repent. Honor your covenant and let God rewrite your marriage—surrender the private things over to Him. 2 Chronicles 7:14 KJV declares, "If my people, which are called by my name, shall humble themselves, and pray, and seek my face, and turn from their wicked ways; then will I hear from heaven, and will forgive their sin, and will heal their land."

Repent and God will forgive. Repent and God will heal your land. Turn to Him and God will heal your heart. Give your marriage over to Christ and He will heal "the land" of your marriage. Trust God, and God will restore you and make your marriage new. David declares in Psalms 51:7 KJV, "Purge me with hyssop, and I shall be clean: wash me, and I shall be whiter than snow."

Let God purge you from the sins of the past. Let God lead your heart. Let God transform you.

Ezekiel 11:19 KJV declares, "And I will give them one heart, and I will put a new spirit within you; and I will take the stony heart out of their flesh, and will give them an heart of flesh:" Let God give you a new heart and a new spirit. Let God wash the borders of your marriage. Start afresh. Start anew. Forgive one another. Move forward. Let God restore you. "There is therefore now no condemnation to them which are in Christ Jesus, who walk not after the flesh, but after the Spirit." Romans 8:1 KJV.

When you repent, He remembers your sin no more. Hebrews 8:12 KJV declares, "For I will be merciful to their unrighteousness, and their sins and their iniquities will I remember no more." Repent and turn to Him. He forgives you. Choose to forgive each other. Choose to forgive yourself. Move forward in unity. Put the past behind you and embrace the new and bright future that God has for you and your family.

## ACTION

- Choose to decide to put away anything that's not like God within the walls of your marriage. Surrender your entire heart to Him.
- Choose to embrace God's Way of doing things and let go of the old pattern.
- Create a family prayer and declare it together daily.

## Day 14

## BEGIN AGAIN

*Therefore if any man be in Christ, he is a new creature: old things are passed away; behold, all things are become new.*

2 CORINTHIANS 5:17 KJV

You can begin again. No matter your past, no matter the circumstance—you can begin again. When you are in Christ, you are a new creature. When you surrender your heart to Christ, old things are passed away, and behold, all things have become new.

When you surrender your marriage to Christ, the old things, old ways, old habits, and old appetites are passed away. Let God transform your marriage. Let God give you a new start. Let God give you a new heart.

According to Strong's Concordance, the Greek word for "New" is "kainos" (G2537), which means "Recently made, fresh, recent, unused, unworn." Let God make every aspect of your marriage brand-new. When you surrender to Christ, He will renew every part of your marriage as if the bondage of the past never happened. Let God soften your heart. Surrender to Christ and let God lead the heart of your marriage.

2 Corinthians 5:17 AMPC declares, "Therefore if any person is [ingrafted] in Christ (the Messiah) he is a new creation (a new creature altogether); the old [previous moral and spiritual condition] has passed away. Behold, the fresh and new has come!"

When you are engrafted in Christ, you are altogether a new creature. In fact, according to 2 Corinthians 5:17 AMPC, when you are in Christ, your old and previous moral and spiritual condition has passed away, and behold, the fresh and the new has come. Let God make your marriage new. Let God make every aspect of your marriage fresh. Let God engraft His Word upon the borders of your heart—surrender your marriage over to Him. "This means that anyone who belongs to Christ has become a new person. The old life is gone; a new life has begun!" 2 Corinthians 5:17 NLT.

Psalms 103:12 KJV declares, "As far as the east is from the west, so far hath he removed our transgressions from us." When you receive and surrender to Christ, He removes the stain of the past from your life. When you surrender to God, He sees you through the Blood of His Son, Jesus Christ—He sees your sin no more.

Psalms 103:12 NLT declares, "He has removed our sins as far from us as the east is from the west." His Blood covers the sins of your past. When you are in Christ, He wipes your slate clean. In Him, you have a fresh start. Choose not to bring up the past. Leave the past behind you and press forward and obtain everything that God has for you both.

Romans 6:1–4 KJV declares, "What shall we say then? Shall we continue in sin, that grace may abound? God forbid. How shall we, that are dead to sin, live any longer therein? Know ye not, that so many of us as were baptized into Jesus Christ were baptized into his death? Therefore we are buried with him by baptism into death: that like as Christ was raised up from the dead by the glory of the Father, even so we also should walk in newness of life."

Let the past go. Choose not to pick up the pain of the past. Choose not to live in the memories of the past. Let the old habits go and walk in the newness of life. You have a choice, you can either live in the bondage of the past or you can walk in the freedom of Christ.

John 8:36 KJV declares, "If the Son therefore shall make you free, ye shall be free indeed." You can choose to be free in Christ or you can stay paralyzed to the bondage of the past. Choose to forgive and free yourself from the bondage of the past. Freedom is a choice. Choose to embrace Christ. Choose to walk in the newness of life. Follow Christ.

"WHAT SHALL we say [to all this]? Are we to remain in sin in order that God's grace (favor and mercy) may multiply and overflow? Certainly not! How can we who died to sin live in it any longer? Are you ignorant of the fact that all of us who have been baptized into Christ Jesus were baptized into His death? We were buried therefore with Him by the baptism into death, so that just as Christ was raised from the dead by the glorious [power] of the Father, so we too might [habitually] live and behave in newness of life." Romans 6:1–4 AMPC.

Choose to habitually walk after the principles and precepts of Christ in every aspect of your marriage. With Christ, you can begin again. With Him, you can start afresh. Leave the dead things in the past and walk forward in unity. Choose to walk forward in Christ. Take it one day at a time and let God order your steps. "The steps of a good man are ordered by the Lord: and he delighteth in his way." Psalms 37:23 KJV.

## ACTION

- Choose not to bring up the past. Let the old things die and choose to embrace the new things of Christ.
- Ask God to send you wise and Godly counselors.
- Pattern yourself after those who pattern themselves after God's Word.
- Guard your heart and language by not bringing up the past as a venomous "emotional dagger."

## Day 15

## ADULTERY

*For by means of a whorish woman a man is brought to a piece of bread:*

PROVERBS 6:26 KJV

When sin enters the borders of your home, it contaminates your destiny. In fact, when unaddressed sin enters the borders of your marriage, it contaminates your generational legacy.

Proverbs 6:26 KJV declares, "For by means of a whorish woman a man is brought to a piece of bread: and the adulteress will hunt for the precious life." The Amplified Version expounds on Proverbs 6:26 AMPC this way, "For on account of a harlot a man is brought to a piece of bread, and the adulteress stalks and snares [as with a hook] the precious life [of a man]." And the New Living Translation declares, "For a prostitute will bring you to poverty, but sleeping with another man's wife will cost you your life." Proverbs 6:26 NLT.

Adultery, both emotional and physical, will cost you. How much is that moment worth? Unaddressed sin will eat away at your destiny. Unaddressed sin will corrode your family from the inside out. Choose to repent and turn from any practices, behaviors, and attitudes that are not like God.

In fact, Jesus declares in Matthew 5:28 KJV, "But I say unto you, That whosoever looketh on a woman to lust after her hath committed adultery with her already in his heart." Who has your heart? Who appeals to any area of your heart? Adultery is not only committed through sex but it is also committed through emotional exchange.

According to 1 Thessalonians 5:23 KJV, we are made up of body, soul, and spirit. "And the very God of peace sanctify you wholly; and I pray God your whole spirit and soul and body be preserved blameless unto the coming of our Lord Jesus Christ." You may be a born again Christian and, your spirit is new in Christ, and you may not have committed physical adultery with your body—but your soul (mind, will, emotions, intellect, and imagination) may be connected to someone else other than your spouse.

Who has access to your heart? Who has access to your soul? "Can a man take fire in his bosom, and his clothes not be burned?" Proverbs 6:27 KJV. Can a man or woman take fire in their bosom and not be burned? Choose to turn away from the temptation of sin. Don't let adultery—emotional or physical—enter into the heart of your marriage.

"And yet they would not hearken unto their judges, but they went a whoring after other gods, and bowed themselves unto them: they turned quickly out of the way which their fathers walked in, obeying the commandments of the Lord; but they did not so." Judges 2:17 KJV. Keep your heart fixed on Christ. Stay focused on God's Way of doing things.

When your heart wanders away from Christ, it begins to wither. When your eye wanders away from your spouse, your marriage begins to wither. Job declares in Job 31:1 AMPC, "I DICTATED a covenant (an agreement) to my eyes; how then could I look [lustfully] upon a girl?" Choose to keep your eyes on your covenant—your spouse.

John 15:1–6 KJV declares, "I am the true vine, and my Father is the husbandman. Every branch in me that beareth not fruit he taketh away: and every branch that beareth fruit, he purgeth it, that it may bring forth more fruit. Now ye are clean through the word which I have spoken unto you. Abide in me, and I in you. As the branch cannot bear fruit of itself, except it abide in the vine; no more can ye, except ye abide in me. I am the vine, ye are the branches: He that abideth in me, and I in him, the same bringeth forth much fruit: for without me ye can do nothing. If a man abide not in me, he is cast forth as a branch, and is withered; and men gather them, and cast them into the fire, and they are burned."

Let your marriage abide in Christ. Surrender your marriage to Christ—the True Vine. When you surrender your marriage to Christ, He will continue to feed and nourish the ground of your heart and home. Let His Word satisfy the heart of your marriage. Let His Word burn away anything that's not like Him. Let His Word prune every area of your heart. Let His Word pierce every area of your marriage.

Let God minister to your heart before He ministers to your marriage. Don't idolize your marriage. Don't idolize your family. Don't idolize or magnify your spouse above God. Choose to serve and surrender to Christ first, and He will lead and show you how to steward the heart of your family and your marriage. "For the lips of a strange woman drop as an honeycomb, and her mouth is smoother than oil: But her end is bitter as wormwood, sharp as a twoedged sword. Her feet go down to death; her steps take hold on hell." Proverbs 5:3–5 KJV.

# ACTION

- Remember, adultery is not only committing the physical or sexual act, but adultery can also be committed through an emotional exchange. Who or what has your heart outside of your marriage? Who or what is your soul tied to?
- Choose not to engage in emotional adultery. Break every ungodly connection outside of your marriage.
- Choose not to engage in flirtatious and other "seemingly" innocent ensnaring behavior. Remember the scripture: Proverbs 5:3–4 KJV "For the lips of a strange woman drop as an honeycomb, and her mouth is smoother than oil: But her end is bitter as wormwood, sharp as a twoedged sword."
- Solely commit your body, heart, mind, and soul to your spouse.
- Pattern yourself after other Godly couples who have patterned themselves after God's Word and His Way of doing things.

# Day 16

## THE WIFE OF THY YOUTH

*Let thy fountain be blessed: and rejoice with the wife of thy youth.*

PROVERBS 5:18 KJV

Let your fountain be blessed. In proper context, the word "fountain", mentioned in Proverbs 5:18 KJV represents your life. Let your life be blessed when you rejoice, honor, and cherish the wife of your youth. In fact, Proverbs 5:18 AMPC expounds on the word, "fountain" further, "Let your fountain [of human life] be blessed [with the rewards of fidelity], and rejoice in the wife of your youth."

There is reward with fidelity. There is peace with fidelity. There is joy in fidelity. Let the fruit of your fidelity fill your house with peace and prosperity. Psalms 147:14 KJV declares, "He maketh peace in thy borders, and filleth thee with the finest of the wheat."

When you choose to obey God and keep His Covenant—He will fill your house with the finest of wheat. In other words, when you obey God, He satisfies you with His best. When you keep His Covenant, He will set your house high above all the nations of the Earth—He will make you an example for generations to follow. Choose to set the Generational Blueprint for others to follow. Obey Christ and keep your Covenant.

Deuteronomy 28:13–14 KJV declares, "And the Lord shall make thee the head, and not the tail; and thou shalt be above only, and thou shalt not be beneath; if that thou hearken unto the commandments of the Lord thy God, which I command thee this day, to observe and to do them: And thou shalt not go aside from any of the words which I command thee this day, to the right hand, or to the left, to go after other gods to serve them."

When you choose to serve other gods, you're committing spiritual adultery. When you choose to break your Covenant with God by serving the lust of your flesh, your heart becomes entangled in the bondage of this world. Choose to keep the fountain of your heart pure.

Proverbs 4:23 KJV declares, "Keep thy heart with all diligence; for out of it are the issues of life." Proverbs 4:23 AMPC expounds on this scripture this way, "Keep and guard your heart with all vigilance and above all that you guard, for out of it flow the springs of life." Diligently guard your heart and your home with His Word. Keep your eyes pure. Keep your mind pure. Keep your thoughts focused on Him.

"Casting down imaginations, and every high thing that exalteth itself against the knowledge of God, and bringing into captivity every thought to the obedience of Christ;" 2 Corinthians 10:5 KJV. Cast down every imagination that exalts itself against your marriage.

According to Strong's Concordance, the Greek word for "Casting Down" is "kathaireō" (G2507), which means "To take down, with the use of force: to throw down, cast down, to pull down, to demolish." Cast down everything that exalts itself against God. Pull down everything that puffs itself up against God's Word.

Be intentional to throw down everything that exalts itself against your marriage. "Because the carnal mind is enmity against God: for it is not subject to the law of God, neither indeed can be." Romans 8:7 KJV. "[That is] because the mind of the flesh [with its carnal thoughts and purposes] is hostile to God, for it does not submit itself to God's Law; indeed it cannot." Romans 8:7 AMPC.

The flesh wars against God. Every thought that's contrary to the Truth of God's Word wars against your marriage. Choose to guard your heart and your fountain with His Word. Men, keep your marriage pure and drink from your own fountain. Women, keep the borders of your marriage clean and undefiled and drink from your own fountain. "Give honor to marriage, and remain faithful to one another in marriage. God will surely judge people who are immoral and those who commit adultery." Hebrews 13:4 NLT

## —— A HUSBAND'S DECLARATION ——

Father God, in the Name of Jesus, I thank You for my wife. Father, I thank You that she satisfies me. Lord, my heart chooses to trust in You. Father, I thank You that my heart safely trusts in her.

Lord, I choose to keep the borders of my heart and house clean. I cast down every imagination and evil thing that exalts itself against our marriage.

Lord, I choose to trust You and demolish any evil thought that attempts to derail our marriage.

Lord, cover my house in Your Word. Lord, cover my house in

Your Blood. There is none like You. Father, I thank You for the opportunity to serve You by leading Your daughter.

Father, lead me. Father, guide my footsteps. Lord, lead my house. Lord, I choose to set the pattern of my home after You.

Lord, create in me a clean heart and renew in me a right spirit—Your Spirit. Lord, I choose to crush every mountain that tries to destroy and crush our marriage.

In the Name of Jesus, I crush every form of lust. Father, I crush every form of idolatry. Lord, our house surrenders to You.

Father, in the Name of Jesus, I crush every generational bondage that tries to hinder our family from moving forward in You.

As the head of the home, I declare, in the Name of Jesus, that every addiction is broken, every stronghold is torn down, every generational cycle is broken, and we surrender our lives to You.

In Jesus' Name. Amen.

## ——— A WIFE'S DECLARATION ———

Father God, in the Name of Jesus, I thank You for my husband. Father, I thank You that he satisfies me. Lord, my heart chooses to trust in You. Father, I thank You that my heart safely trusts in him.

Lord, I choose to keep the borders of my heart and house clean. I cast down every imagination and evil thing that exalts itself against our marriage.

Lord, I choose to trust You and demolish any evil thought that attempts to derail our marriage.

Lord, cover my house in Your Word. Lord, cover my house in Your Blood. There is none like You.

Father, lead our house. Father, guide our footsteps. Lord, we choose to set the pattern of our home after Your Word.

Lord, create in me a clean heart and renew in me a right spirit—Your Spirit. Lord, I choose to crush every mountain that tries to destroy and crush our marriage.

In the Name of Jesus, I crush every form of lust. Father, I crush every form of idolatry. In the Name of Jesus, I crush every form of perversion. Lord, our house surrenders to You.

Father, in the Name of Jesus, I crush every generational bondage that tries to hinder our family from moving forward in You.

I declare, in the Name of Jesus, that every addiction is broken, every stronghold is torn down, every generational cycle is crushed, and we surrender our lives to You.

In Jesus' Name. Amen.

# Day 17

# ICHABOD

*And she named the child I–chabod, saying,*
*The glory is departed from Israel: because the*
*ark of God was taken, and because of her father*
*in law and her husband.*

1 SAMUEL 4:21 KJV

According to Strong's Concordance, the Hebrew word for "Ichabod" is "Iy-kabowd" (H350), which means "No glory." Isn't it interesting that this mother would name her child, "Ichabod"? Why would a mother assign such a name to her child? Why would she assign such a devastating name to something that she gave birth to? As previously mentioned, "Ichabod" means "No glory." Think about this concept for a moment; a mother who carries a child in her womb for nine months, and then finally gives birth to a new born baby, decides to assign the name, "No glory." Let's look behind the scenes and examine this interesting account outlined in 1 Samuel 4:15–22 KJV:

"Now Eli was ninety and eight years old; and his eyes were dim, that he could not see." 1 Samuel 4:15 KJV

"And the man said unto Eli, I am he that came out of the army, and I fled to day out of the army. And he said, What is there done, my son?" 1 Samuel 4:16 KJV

"And the messenger answered and said, Israel is fled before the Philistines, and there hath been also a great slaughter among the people, and thy two sons also, Hophni and Phinehas, are dead, and the ark of God is taken." 1 Samuel 4:17 KJV

"And it came to pass, when he made mention of the ark of God, that he fell from off the seat backward by the side of the gate, and his neck brake, and he died: for he was an old man, and heavy. And he had judged Israel forty years." 1 Samuel 4:18 KJV

"And his daughter in law, Phinehas' wife, was with child, near to be delivered: and when she heard the tidings that the ark of God was taken, and that her father in law and her husband were dead, she bowed herself and travailed; for her pains came upon her." 1 Samuel 4:19 KJV

"And about the time of her death the women that stood by her said unto her, Fear not; for thou hast born a son. But she answered not, neither did she regard it." 1 Samuel 4:20 KJV

"And she named the child I-chabod, saying, The glory is departed from Israel: because the ark of God was taken, and because of her father in law and her husband." 1 Samuel 4:21 KJV

"And she said, The glory is departed from Israel: for the ark of God is taken." 1 Samuel 4:22 KJV

So now the story begins to unfold. We can see in 1 Samuel 4:17 KJV that Eli, the lead priest and judge at the time, received the bad report that his two sons, Hophni and Phinehas, had died and the Philistines had also captured the Ark of the Covenant. When Eli received this devastating news that the Philistines had invaded Israel and killed his legacy—according to 1 Samuel 4:18, Eli died as well.

According to Strong's Concordance, the Hebrew word for "Philistine" is "Plishtiy" (H6430), which means "Immigrants." What uncircumcised Philistine has migrated onto the borders of your camp? What uncircumcised Philistine has migrated into the borders of your marriage? What Philistine has illegally taken up residence in your home? Who or what is trying to steal your peace? Guard your heart and protect your peace from anyone or anything that tries to infiltrate the ground of your heart and marriage.

According to Strong's Concordance, the Hebrew word for "Phinehas" is "Piynchac" (H6372), which means "Mouth of brass" or "the mouth of a serpent." According to Strong's Concordance, the Hebrew word for "Hophni" is "Chophniy" (H2652), which means "Pugilist (A boxer)." The two sons of Eli served as priests, and both were violent, corrupt, and lustful.

In other words, sin entered Israel's camp through their priesthood, the sons of Eli—Phinehas and Hophni. When sin entered, these activities remained unchecked by the head priest and judge, Eli. An unchecked culture of sin will open the door to the enemy. When sin enters your home, choose to address it. God will give you the wisdom to address the culture of sin in your family.

An unchecked heart or an unrepentant heart opens the door for the enemy to take dominion. Eli, who was the head priest and judge of Israel, was passive and did not check his sons. In fact, he allowed the corruption to grow. Eli created an environment in his home for the enemy to gain access, reign, and to take dominion. The death of his sons was the physical manifestation of what was happening internally. God allowed the Philistines, a foreign enemy, to invade Israel because of what was happening behind closed doors. What's happening within the borders of your home? What's happening behind the closed doors of your marriage?

1 Samuel 4:1–2 KJV declares, "And the word of Samuel came to all Israel. Now Israel went out against the Philistines to battle, and pitched beside Eben–ezer: and the Philistines pitched in Aphek. And the Philistines put themselves in array against Israel: and when they joined battle, Israel was smitten before the Philistines: and they slew of the army in the field about four thousand men."

The first time Israel went to battle against the enemy—four thousand men were killed by the hand of the Philistines. You can't defeat the enemy when your heart and hands are corrupt. "Draw nigh to God, and he will draw nigh to you. Cleanse your hands, ye sinners; and purify your hearts, ye double minded." James 4:8 KJV

Later in 1 Samuel 4:3–4 NLT, "After the battle was over, the troops retreated to their camp, and the elders of Israel asked, "Why did the Lord allow us to be defeated by the Philistines?" Then they said, "Let's bring the Ark of the Covenant of the Lord from Shiloh. If we carry it into battle with us, it will save us from our enemies." So they sent men to Shiloh to bring the Ark of the Covenant of the Lord of Heaven's Armies, who is enthroned between the cherubim. Hophni and Phinehas, the sons of Eli, were also there with the Ark of the Covenant of God."

After the Israelites were defeated by the Philistines for the first time, the Israelites regrouped. Notice, in 1 Samuel 4:3–4 NLT, Israel decided to go back to their old spiritual strategy that had previously helped them win wars in the past. The Israelites went back to retrieve the Ark of the Covenant and the priests. They knew that if God was with them, as in past times, they would win the battle.

Notice in 1 Samuel 4:1 KJV, the Israelites fought without the Ark of the Covenant, and they went back to go get the Presence of God—the Ark of the Covenant. The first time Israel went to battle, they went to war in their own flesh. They went to war without the Ark of the Covenant. Look at the outcome—Israel was defeated. The lesson—don't battle the enemy without God. Don't go to war without His Word. You can't win a spiritual battle with carnal weaponry. Don't go to war in your own strength. Apply His Word to every part of your life, family, and marriage.

Don't cherry pick or "self-select" the Word of God. Don't only apply the part of the Word that's convenient for you. Notice, that is exactly what the Israelites did—they used the Power of God, the Ark of the Covenant, when it was convenient for them. When they went to war the first time and saw themselves losing against the Philistines—they retreated and sought God.

Married couples, it's ok to retreat and seek God's Counsel in order to readjust your strategy against the enemy—but it's pointless if you retreat and don't repent. Retreating without repentance will keep you in the same cycle.

In 1 Samuel 4:5 NLT, look at what happened to the children of Israel, "When all the Israelites saw the Ark of the Covenant of the Lord coming into the camp, their shout of joy was so loud it made the ground shake!" Isn't this how we behave when we go to church on Sunday, read a Bible passage or read a Bible-based book?

For a season, you're strengthened on the outside and you're excited about what God can do "for" you instead of doing the internal "heart work" and letting God transform you from the inside out. The Israelites were happy on the outside but on the inside, they had no power. Let God transform you from the inside out.

When the Philistines heard the Israelites shout because they had got a hold of the Ark of the Covenant—the Philistines, at first, were afraid—as they should have been. But remember, there was one problem—God was not with the Israelites.

Although the Israelites had the physical possession of the Ark of the Covenant, on the outside, the Israelites looked like they had power—but on the inside, God had left them. The Israelites had turned their hearts away from God, and as a result, they were powerless.

On the outside, powerless couples look like they have it together—but on the inside, they have no power. Choose to repent and turn back to God. What's happening within the borders of your heart? What's happening within the borders of your home? What's happening within the borders of your marriage? What happens privately—God will expose publicly.

Back to Ichabod. So after Eli's daughter-in-law, Phinehas's wife, heard the news of the death of her husband, Phinehas and her father-in-law, Eli, notice what happened to her emotional condition in 1 Samuel 4:19 KJV, "And his daughter in law, Phinehas' wife, was with child, near to be delivered: and when she heard the tidings that the ark of God was taken, and that her father in law and her husband were dead, she bowed herself and travailed; for her pains came upon her."

1 Samuel 4:19 NLT puts it this way, "Eli's daughter-in-law, the wife of Phinehas, was pregnant and near her time of delivery. When she heard that the Ark of God had been captured and that her father-in-law and husband were dead, she went into labor and gave birth."

When she heard of this devastating news, she travailed. She gave birth to pain. In fact, according to 1 Samuel 4:20 KJV she was hopeless to the point of death. Don't let the pain of the past lord over your future. Don't let the pain of the past lord over your marriage. Forgive yourself. Forgive others. Forgive freely and keep moving forward.

Look at how fear and hopelessness gripped Phinehas's wife in 1 Samuel 4:20 KJV, "And about the time of her death the women that stood by her said unto her, Fear not; for thou hast born a son. But she answered not, neither did she regard it." In Bible days, typically, when a son was born to a Hebrew family, the occasion was celebrated with great joy. A son represented legacy, and he would carry the family's name. A child brought great joy and glory to a family.

However, look at Phinehas's wife response in 1 Samuel 4:20 NLT, "She died in childbirth, but before she passed away the midwives tried to encourage her. "Don't be afraid," they said. "You have a baby boy!" But she did not answer or pay attention to them." Notice what happened to Phinehas's wife in 1 Samuel 4:20 NLT, she did not answer or pay attention to them. She became bitter and indifferent.

When you hold on to the pain of the past, you become bitter and indifferent. When you hold on to the condemnation, bitterness, and regret of the past, your heart begins to harden and you eventually grow cold. Let God soften your heart. Let God lead your heart. Let the past go. Forgive and let God turn your heart around. Forgive and let God turn your marriage around. Turn your heart to Him. Don't grow cold. Turn to Him.

Bitterness will keep your family in cycles for generations. Look at what happened in 1 Samuel 4:21 KJV, "And she named the child I-chabod, saying, The glory is departed from Israel: because the ark of God was taken, and because of her father in law and her husband." She named her child, "I-chabod," based upon her temporary emotional pain, she assigned a permanent declaration over her seed based upon tragedies that happened in the past. You can't heal if you keep focusing on the past. You can't heal if you keep holding on to the past. She gave life to a perpetual generational cycle.

What are you giving life to? What are you improperly naming? Remember, "Death and life are in the power of the tongue: and they that love it shall eat the fruit thereof." Proverbs 18:21 KJV. She chose to name her child—Ichabod, "No glory." Her confession revealed the condition of her heart. Don't let your temporary pain contaminate the ground of your heart.

Your words are seeds that spring up from the ground of your heart. Let God renew the fountain of your marriage. Let God renew the fountain of your family. Let your words reflect His Heart.

Even on this woman's death bed, she held on to her personal perverted confession that the glory had left Israel—when in fact, this was not true. 1 Samuel 2:35 KJV declares, "And I will raise me up a faithful priest, that shall do according to that which is in mine heart and in my mind: and I will build him a sure house; and he shall walk before mine anointed for ever."

Her vision was skewed based upon her emotional condition. Her vision was shortsighted. Her confession was short-lived. The glory was still in Israel—it just shifted from her house. God had raised up a faithful priest—Samuel, whose name means, "Heard of God."

God hears you. God hears your cry. Choose to cry out to Him. 1 Peter 5:7 KJV declares, "Casting all your care upon him; for he careth for you." Cast your cares to Him. Don't let the weight of the past lord over your future. In fact, according to Strong's Concordance, the Hebrew word for "Glory" is "kabowd" (H3519), which means "Honor, weight, splendor, reputation."

Let His Word and His Way have more weight in your life. Let His Word and His Way have more weight in your marriage. Let the bondage of the past go. Let His Way have more weight than your present emotional condition.

Remember, if you ever feel that the glory has left your marriage or if your current pain is so weighty that it perverts your vision and twists your confession—choose to remember that God's weight is mightier than your problem.

God hears you, and He is for you. Forgive, repent, and embrace God's future for your marriage. His Way is weightier than your past. Let God rewrite every aspect of your heart. Let God rewrite every aspect of your marriage.

## ACTION

- Choose your words wisely; as stated in Proverbs 18:21 KJV, death and life are in the power of your tongue. Today, choose your words wisely. Decide to continually speak life over your marriage.

- Forgive yourself. Forgive your spouse. Forgive others who have trespassed against you.

- Remember, God is mightier and stronger than any problem that you may face.

- Choose to surrender to God and cast your cares, worries, anxieties, and fears over to God continually.

# Day 18

# THE YOKE BREAKER

*And it shall come to pass in that day, that his burden shall be taken away from off thy shoulder, and his yoke from off thy neck, and the yoke shall be destroyed because of the anointing.*

ISAIAH 10:27 KJV

Jesus Christ is the Yoke Breaker. He is the Cycle Breaker. There is no generational curse that He cannot break. There is no generational cycle that He cannot destroy. There is no generational barrier that He cannot obliterate. It does not matter what bondage, addiction, struggle, or stronghold that has your family bound—Jesus Christ came to break you free from every bondage and trap of the enemy.

Matthew 4:1–11 KJV outlines how Jesus Christ was tempted by the enemy and defeated every aspect of the wilderness for you. The wilderness was designed to distract you. The wilderness was designed to drain you. The wilderness was designed to ensnare you. The wilderness was designed to starve you.

If you're ever faced with a wilderness season—remember that God is bigger than the wilderness that you face. Don't let the wilderness overtake you. If you're ever faced with a wilderness season in your life or within the walls of your marriage, be determined to surrender to Christ. Choose to build with Christ. God is greater than the wilderness that you face. Choose to yield to Christ and let God lead you out of the wilderness.

Let's examine what the Bible declares about wilderness seasons. Matthew 4:1–2 KJV states, "Then was Jesus led up of the Spirit into the wilderness to be tempted of the devil. And when he had fasted forty days and forty nights, he was afterward an hungred."

Notice the following words outlined in Matthew 4:1 KJV: "Jesus was led." Whenever you face a wilderness or dry season, always refer to His Word. Notice in this passage, the Bible declares that "Jesus was led" into the wilderness. Remember that God saw the wilderness before it formed. The wilderness or dry season did not catch God by surprise. God sees you. God knows what you're dealing with. He knows your struggles. He knows your pain. He knows you intimately. God is greater than any wilderness that you may face. His Power is stronger than any grip of the enemy. Don't magnify the wilderness over God's authority. Surrender to Christ and know that He will lead you out of the wilderness and out of every dry place.

Notice the next point about the wilderness in Matthew 4:1 KJV, "... to be tempted ..." The enemy wants to tempt you in the wilderness. The enemy wants to derail your destiny. When you are in Christ, He has given you the strength and authority to conquer the power of the enemy. Don't yield to temptation, yield to Christ. Jesus Christ has set the pattern for us to follow. He conquered every temptation that the enemy threw at Him. Jesus conquered every aspect of the wilderness. He crushed every cycle for you.

This is what Jesus declares in Luke 10:19 KJV about the power of the enemy, "Behold, I give unto you power to tread on serpents and scorpions, and over all the power of the enemy: and nothing shall by any means hurt you." His Word will always triumph over the enemy. When you are in Christ, the wilderness cannot defeat you. When you are in Him, the wilderness cannot destroy you. God has given you the power to conquer the enemy in every area of your life. When you are in Christ, the wilderness, or the things in it, cannot harm you. God has given you the power to overthrow the enemy in every area of your life. God has given you the power to overthrow the enemy in every area of your family. God has given you the power to crush and overthrow the enemy in every area of your marriage.

Let's examine another point in Matthew 4:2 KJV, ". . . And when he had fasted forty days and forty nights . . ." The wilderness has a time limit. The wilderness is temporary. Remember that the enemy wants you to magnify the wilderness season. Remember that the wilderness is just that—a season. The enemy wants you to amplify the events, tests, and trials in the wilderness. The enemy wants you to think that the wilderness is bigger than what it is. God is greater than any season that you may face. God is in control and Satan must bow to God's Authority.

In fact, look at what the Bible declares in Job 1:6–11 KJV: "Now there was a day when the sons of God came to present themselves before the Lord, and Satan came also among them. And the Lord said unto Satan, Whence comest thou? Then Satan answered the Lord, and said, From going to and fro in the earth, and from walking up and down in it. And the Lord said unto Satan, Hast thou considered my servant Job, that there is none like him in the earth, a perfect and an upright man, one that feareth God, and escheweth evil? Then Satan answered the Lord, and said, Doth Job fear God for nought? Hast not thou made an hedge about him, and about his house, and about all that he hath on every side? thou hast blessed the work of his hands, and his substance is increased in the land. But put forth thine hand now, and touch all that he hath, and he will curse thee to thy face."

Let's examine the following passage in Job 1:10–11 KJV: "Hast not thou made an hedge about him, and about his house, and about all that he hath on every side? thou hast blessed the work of his hands, and his substance is increased in the land. But put forth thine hand now, and touch all that he hath, and he will curse thee to thy face." Notice what Satan declares about Job in Job 1:10 AMPC, "Have You not put a hedge about him and his house and all that he has, on every side? You have conferred prosperity and happiness upon him in the work of his hands, and his possessions have increased in the land."

Satan saw the hedge that God had made around Job, his house, family, and his possessions. Satan could not have access to Job, nor could he touch anything that belonged to Job—without God's permission. The protection of God or the "Hand of God" covered Job and all that he had. When you are in Christ, the enemy cannot touch you without God's permission.

Isaiah 54:17 AMPC declares, "But no weapon that is formed against you shall prosper, and every tongue that shall rise against you in judgment you shall show to be in the wrong. This [peace, righteousness, security, triumph over opposition] is the heritage of the servants of the Lord [those in whom the ideal Servant of the Lord is reproduced]; this is the righteousness or the vindication which they obtain from Me [this is that which I impart to them as their justification], says the Lord." No weapon, strategy, plot, or scheme that the enemy forms can stop you. Let His Word establish the borders of your house. Let His Blood cover the inner workings of your family. Let God lead every aspect of your heart. Let God lead every aspect of your marriage.

## COUPLES' PRAYER

Father God, in the Name of Jesus, we thank You for our marriage. Father, we thank You for the Blood of Your Son—Jesus Christ.

We thank You that His Blood covers our hearts. Father, we thank You that the Blood of Jesus Christ covers every aspect of our marriage.

Father, thank You for setting a hedge around our family. Thank You for blessing the work of our hands. Thank You for leading us through every season of life.

Thank You for breaking every wilderness cycle. Thank You for breaking every generational curse and cycle through the shed Blood of Jesus Christ.

Father, there is no one like You. Lord, our family surrenders to You. Father, in You every yoke is broken. Father, through Your Son Jesus Christ, we are set free from every torment, entanglement, stronghold, bitterness, and disease.

Lord, we surrender our hearts to You. Lord, we redirect our hearts toward You. Father, we surrender to You now and forever. Lord, rewrite our story.

In Jesus' Name. Amen.

## Day 19

## THE LORD IS
## MY SHEPHERD

*The Lord is my shepherd;
I shall not want.*

PSALMS 23:1 KJV

Let the Lord lead your family. Back in Biblical times, a shepherd was one who was responsible for leading, guarding, and protecting a flock of animals—oftentimes, they led sheep. When the Lord is your Shepherd, He is responsible for leading, guarding, and protecting your family. When you surrender your heart to Christ, He is the One who is responsible for directing your family's footsteps. Let God lead, order, and direct the steps of your marriage.

Psalm 23:1 AMPC declares, "THE Lord is my Shepherd [to feed, guide, and shield me], I shall not lack." There is no lack in Him. Let the Lord feed you. Let the Lord guide you. Let the Lord shield you. Let the Lord protect the heart of your marriage. When the Lord leads you, there is no spiritual lack in Him. When the Lord leads you, there is no emotional lack in Him. When the Lord leads you, there is no financial lack in Him. In Him, there is no lack. Choose to add this scripture to your family's declaration: "The Lord is my shepherd; I have all that I need." Psalms 23:1 NLT.

## SURRENDER TO CHRIST

"He maketh me to lie down in green pastures: he leadeth me beside the still waters." Psalms 23:2 KJV.

He causes me to rest. The Lord will cause you to rest and to be at peace. Let the Lord fill the borders of your family with His Peace. Psalms 23:2 NLT declares, "He lets me rest in green meadows; he leads me beside peaceful streams." Let His Word lead your marriage beside peaceful streams. Let His Word nourish the heart of your marriage.

Matthew 4:4 KJV declares, "But he answered and said, It is written, Man shall not live by bread alone, but by every word that proceedeth out of the mouth of God." Let your marriage be satisfied by His Word. Let the soil of your marriage be nourished by His Word. Psalm 23:2 AMPC declares, "He makes me lie down in [fresh, tender] green pastures; He leads me beside the still and restful waters." May His Word be fresh, tender, and relevant to every area of your marriage.

When you surrender to Christ and allow His Way and His Word to nourish and satisfy the heart of your marriage, He will restore your soul. Psalms 23:3 KJV declares, "He restoreth my soul: he leadeth me in the paths of righteousness for his name's sake." The New Living Translation expounds upon Psalms 23:3 NLT in the following manner, "He renews my strength. He guides me along right paths, bringing honor to his name."

Let the Lord renew your strength. Let the Lord renew the

strength of your marriage. Let His Power penetrate and refresh every aspect of your marriage. Psalm 23:3 AMPC declares, "He refreshes and restores my life (my self); He leads me in the paths of righteousness [uprightness and right standing with Him–not for my earning it, but] for His name's sake." Let His Word lead your marriage in the paths of righteousness.

When you surrender your heart, your family, and your marriage over to Christ, He will stabilize your path and cause you to be in right standing with Him. Let God stabilize you. Let God refresh you. Let God lead you and set you on the right path.

## FEAR NO EVIL

"Yea, though I walk through the valley of the shadow of death, I will fear no evil: for thou art with me; thy rod and thy staff they comfort me." Psalms 23:4 KJV.

Psalms 23:4 NLT declares, "Even when I walk through the darkest valley, I will not be afraid, for you are close beside me. Your rod and your staff protect and comfort me." No matter the season, no matter the valley—remember that God is with you. As a couple, you may face dark valleys and dry seasons—choose to remember that God is with you. Remember that God is close beside you, and He will never leave you or forsake you. When the pressures of life try to shake you and emotional obstacles try to overtake you—remember that God is with you and nothing can defeat you.

Notice what Psalms 23:4 KJV declares, "Yea, though I walk through the valley of the shadow of death . . ." The shadow of death is just that—a shadow. Choose to magnify God over the shadows that you face. Magnify God over your circumstance. There is no valley that's greater than God. There's no emotional pit that's greater than God. God is greater than depression. God is greater than any oppression that tries to weigh you down. God is greater than the shadows that you face.

Psalms 91:1–2 KJV declares, "He that dwelleth in the secret place of the most High shall abide under the shadow of the Almighty. I will say of the Lord, He is my refuge and my fortress: my God; in him will I trust." Dwell in God's shadow. God's shadow is greater than the shadow of the valley. His covering protects you. His covering shields you. His rod and His staff comforts you. Walk through the valley—with God. Choose to focus on God and not the darkness of the valley. "Yes, though I walk through the [deep, sunless] valley of the shadow of death, I will fear or dread no evil, for You are with me; Your rod [to protect] and Your staff [to guide], they comfort me." Psalm 23:4 AMPC.

## HE PREPARES A TABLE BEFORE ME

"Thou preparest a table before me in the presence of mine enemies: thou anointest my head with oil; my cup runneth over." Psalms 23:5 KJV.

According to Strong's Concordance, the Hebrew word for "Preparest" is "arak" (H6186), which means "To arrange, set or put or lay in order, set in array, prepare, order, ordain, handle, furnish, esteem, equal, direct, compare." When you surrender your heart and your marriage to God—He prepares, arranges, sets in order a table before you in the presence of your enemies.

Actually, the word "Prepareth" has an "-eth" on the end of it, which means "to continue." God continues to arrange a table for you and your family in the presence of your enemies. Keep your eyes fixed on God. Surrender to Him. Keep your eyes focused on His Way of doing things. He's anointed you to do this. He's prepared you to do this.

Psalms 23:5 NLT declares, "You prepare a feast for me in the presence of my enemies. You honor me by anointing my head with oil. My cup overflows with blessings." Let God continually prepare a feast for you and your family. There is no lack in Him. There is no confusion in Him. When God prepares a table for you, it is without the permission of your enemies. Let God do it.

Let God prepare the table and let your family feast on His Goodness. Let your family feast on His Faithfulness. Don't focus on your enemies—focus on God. Obey His Word and let God prepare your feast. Don't focus on the naysayers—focus on God. Don't focus on your problems—focus on God. Don't focus on the valley—focus on God. Don't focus on the waves and winds of life—focus on God. Focus on the feast that God is preparing. God is preparing your victory.

## ANOINT MY HEAD WITH OIL. MY CUP RUNS OVER

After God prepares a feast before you in the presence of your enemies, the next part of Psalms 23:5 AMPC declares, ". . . You anoint my head with oil; my [brimming] cup runs over." Let God anoint your head with oil. According to Strong's Concordance, the Hebrew word for "Anoint" is "dashen" (H1878), which means

"To be fat, grow fat, become fat, become prosperous, to take away ashes (from altar), to fatten oneself (of Jehovah's sword)."

Let God anoint your head with oil. Let God smear you with His oil. Let God anoint you. Let God anoint your family. Let your family grow fat in His Word. Let your house become prosperous by surrendering to His Word. Let your house grow and expand by surrendering to His Word. Let God take away the guilt, shame, defeat, and bondage of the past. Let God anoint your family with His oil.

Notice the next phrase in Psalms 23:5 KJV, "You anoint my head." Let God anoint the head of your house. According to Strong's Concordance, the Hebrew word for "Head" is "ro'sh" (H7218), which means "Head, top, summit, upper part, chief, total, sum, height, front, beginning."

Let God anoint the head of your family. Let God anoint the beginning of your marriage. Let God anoint every aspect of your marriage—from beginning to the ending. Let God anoint the chief part of your ministry. Your family is your ministry. Your marriage is your ministry. Let God anoint the total sum of your family. Let God anoint your mind to receive the Word of God.

Let God anoint your hands to apply the Word of God to every part of your life. Let God anoint your footsteps to follow His instruction. Let God anoint your family. Let the cup of your family overflow with His oil. When the head is anointed—the rest of the family benefits.

Walk in obedience. Submit to God and surely His Goodness, and Mercy shall follow the legacy of your family forever.

# SURELY GOODNESS AND MERCY SHALL FOLLOW ME

"Surely goodness and mercy shall follow me all the days of my life: and I will dwell in the house of the Lord for ever." Psalms 23:6 KJV.

Psalms 23:6 NLT declares, "Surely your goodness and unfailing love will pursue me all the days of my life, and I will live in the house of the Lord forever." Let the unfailing Love of God pursue you and your family all the days of your life. Let God erase your past. Choose to embrace the newness of God. Let your family dwell in the house of the Lord forever.

Let His Peace overtake you. Let His Mercy undergird you. Let your family dwell in peace. Let your family reflect the Heart of God. Let your marriage dwell in His House forever. Let your marriage be protected by the goodness, mercy, and unfailing love of God. Let His Power protect you. Let His Peace guide your footsteps. Let His Peace and His Presence lead and establish the generational pattern for generations to come. Let your house surrender to God.

## ACTION

- Declare the entire chapter of Psalms 23 out loud with your family.
- Choose to be the difference. Let God lead your home.

# Day 20

## MAKE ROOM

*And it fell on a day, that Elisha passed to Shunem, where was a great woman; and she constrained him to eat bread. And so it was, that as oft as he passed by, he turned in thither to eat bread.*

2 KINGS 4:8 KJV

*And she said unto her husband, Behold now, I perceive that this is an holy man of God, which passeth by us continually.*

2 KINGS 4:9 KJV

*Let us make a little chamber, I pray thee, on the wall; and let us set for him there a bed, and a table, and a stool, and a candlestick: and it shall be, when he cometh to us, that he shall turn in thither.*

2 KINGS 4:10 KJV

*And it fell on a day, that he came thither, and he turned into the chamber, and lay there.*

2 KINGS 4:11 KJV

*And he said to Gehazi his servant, Call this Shunammite. And when he had called her, she stood before him.*

2 KINGS 4:12 KJV

*And he said unto him, Say now unto her, Behold, thou hast been careful for us with all this care; what is to be done for thee? wouldest thou be spoken for to the king, or to the captain of the host? And she answered, I dwell among mine own people.*

2 KINGS 4:13 KJV

*And he said, What then is to be done for her? And Gehazi answered, Verily she hath no child, and her husband is old.*

2 KINGS 4:14 KJV

*And he said, Call her. And when he had called her, she stood in the door.*

2 KINGS 4:15 KJV

*And he said, About this season, according to the time of life, thou shalt embrace a son. And she said, Nay, my lord, thou man of God, do not lie unto thine handmaid.*

2 KINGS 4:16 KJV


*And the woman conceived, and bare a son at that season that Elisha had said unto her, according to the time of life.*

2 KINGS 4:17 KJV

According to 2 Kings 4:8–11 KJV, Elisha made frequent trips through a city called "Shunem." The Hebrew word "Shunem" (H7766) means "Double resting place." Elisha was passing through the "double resting place."

As Elisha passed through the "double resting place," the Bible declares that "a great woman" noticed that Elisha frequently passed through the city and urged him to eat. This "great woman" invited Elisha into her home to eat and to rest as Elisha passed through the city.

Elisha, who was a man of God, who carried the Word of God was invited into this woman's home. Notice that the Bible refers to this woman as "great." In this instance, the Bible uses the word "great" to describe this woman's influence, status, and wealth.

Although this woman was considered "great" she did not allow her greatness, popularity, influence or stature to block her from hosting the man of God. She was intentional and took the time to invite Elisha into her home to eat and rest.

Proverbs 1:20 AMPC declares, "Wisdom cries aloud in the street, she raises her voice in the markets;" Wisdom cries in the streets or wisdom cries in the common places—those who are wise can recognize when wisdom is crying in the streets.

As Elisha was passing through the streets, this great Shunammite woman decided to let Elisha into her home. Married couples, be intentional to let wisdom in. Allow wisdom, the Word of God, to rule, rest, abide, and dwell within the intimate borders of your home. Choose to let wisdom dwell within the borders of your family and marriage.

In 2 Kings 4:9 KJV, the Shunammite woman did something else very peculiar. 2 Kings 4:9 KJV declares, "And she said unto her husband, Behold now, I perceive that this is an holy man of God, which passeth by us continually."

Notice, although this Shunammite woman was considered "great." She perceived that Elisha was a "Holy man of God." She did not idolize her "greatness." Her influence, wealth, and stature did not "lord" over her. In fact, she submitted to the counsel of her husband. Although she had influence and she was considered "great" within the walls of the city, she honored and submitted to her husband. In fact, they both submitted one to another.

**Let's examine a few Biblical principles that this powerful married couple exemplified in this passage:**

- **Submission:** "Submitting yourselves one to another in the fear of God." Ephesians 5:21 KJV. This married couple saw that the man of God, Elisha, had a need. No one forced them to utilize their resources. No one forced them to open up their home. They soberly discussed the matter between each other and agreed upon how they were going to utilize their resources. They honored each other by listening to the thoughts, plans, and opinions of one another. Ultimately they executed together—in unity.

- **Honor:** "Wives, submit yourselves unto your own husbands, as unto the Lord." Ephesians 5:22 KJV. Submission is not slavery. Submission is unity. When a well-oiled family is fitly framed together, nothing can stop a house that decides to move forward together in agreement. Submission is a sign of honor. Submission is an intentional choice. Rebellion is a sign of immaturity and insecurity. A house that submits to the Word will flourish.

- **Agreement:** "Can two walk together, except they be agreed?" Amos 3:3 KJV Jesus said it best in Matthew 12:25 KJV, ". . . Every kingdom divided against itself is brought to desolation; and every city or house divided against itself shall not stand." God blessed the house of this Shunammite woman and of her husband because of their obedience, humility, and agreement.

Let God Bless your home through your obedience, submission, honor, and agreement. Come together and honor God through every aspect of your marriage.

Let's expound a little more on the next scripture. 2 Kings 4:10 KJV states, "Let us make a little chamber, I pray thee, on the wall; and let us set for him there a bed, and a table, and a stool, and a candlestick: and it shall be, when he cometh to us, that he shall turn in thither."

Another principle noted in 2 Kings 4:10 KJV is what the Shunammite woman declares to her husband. She suggests the following to her husband, "Let us make a little chamber." Let's focus on the first part of this statement, "Let us." What a powerful statement! This statement, "Let us," also points to the wisdom of this Shunammite woman. Instead of manipulating her husband, she simply submitted to his authority and honored him by making this holy request.

Like Queen Esther, who also had authority, submitted to her husband, the king, and made her petition known. Choose to honor your marriage by submitting and surrendering your thoughts, ideas, plans, and strategies to God together. Let God lead your path. Let God lead your words.

This Shunammite woman chose to honor God through submission. Submission brings about honor. The statement, "let us," also points to her ability to lead a team and her ability to influence key decision makers and stakeholders.

"Let us" is an excellent example of how "great" leaders incorporate the feedback of those around them, below them, and those who are above them. Although the Shunammite woman was considered a "great" woman outside of the home, inside of the home she submitted to the authority of her husband—not as a means of bondage but from the position of honor. Great leaders submit to those above them, around them, and those who are beneath them. Choose to serve with others well. Choose to honor well. Choose to lead well, and God will bless the work of your hands.

Let's continue, 2 Kings 4:10 KJV declares, "Let us make a little chamber, I pray thee, on the wall; and let us set for him there a bed, and a table, and a stool, and a candlestick: and it shall be, when he cometh to us, that he shall turn in thither." The married couple made room for Elisha to dwell. Married couples, make your house a permanent dwelling place for God's Presence to dwell.

This married couple made the conscious decision to create an environment for the man of God to dwell whenever he passed by. Married couples, create an atmosphere in the borders of your home where God can dwell and move freely within the walls of your home and marriage. Set the atmosphere. Pray together. Sing together. Worship together. Read the Bible together. Create an atmosphere that invites the Holy Spirit to rest and dwell freely. Be intentional to surrender to the Will of God like this Shunammite couple.

Let's move on to the next scripture, 2 Kings 4:11–12 KJV declares, "And it fell on a day, that he came thither, and he turned into the chamber, and lay there. And he said to Gehazi his servant, Call this Shunammite. And when he had called her, she stood before him." Notice that this is a critical part of Elisha's encounter. The Bible declares that Elisha became comfortable, and one day, he called her into his chambers.

Don't simply skip over this part of the verse! Elisha and his servant, Gehazi, "called in" the Shunammite woman. Remember that this was the Shunammite woman's house and Elisha "called her" into the room! This is another example of the Shunammite woman's humility and how much they honored and respected the man of God.

When Elisha summoned the Shunammite woman through Gehazi, his servant, she submitted to Elisha's call and responded to the man of God. Choose to submit to God and His Way of doing things, and God will establish your borders.

One of the many lessons that we can learn from this Shunammite woman is that she willingly submitted to the man of God. She laid aside her carnal authority, influence, and earthly greatness—and surrendered to Heaven's authority. Lay aside your crown, wealth, influence, authority, and earthly position and surrender to God.

Let's continue. 2 Kings 4:13 KJV declares, "And he said unto him, Say now unto her, Behold, thou hast been careful for us with all this care; what is to be done for thee? wouldest thou be spoken for to the king, or to the captain of the host? And she answered, I dwell among mine own people."

Notice what Elisha declares unto the Shunammite woman in 2 Kings 4:13 AMPC, "And he said to Gehazi, Say now to her, You have been most painstakingly and reverently concerned for us; what is to be done for you? Would you like to be spoken for to the king or to the commander of the army? She answered, I dwell among my own people [they are sufficient]." In other words, Elisha asked the Shunammite woman, "What's your motive?" Notice the Shunammite woman's response—she had no motive. She had no ill intent. She was satisfied. She just wanted to honor and treat the man of God well! She had clean hands and a pure heart.

**Notice these key principles:**

- **Promotion Comes From God:** "Who shall ascend into the hill of the Lord? or who shall stand in his holy place? He that hath clean hands, and a pure heart; who hath not lifted up his soul unto vanity, nor sworn deceitfully." Psalms 24:3-4 KJV. Keep your hands clean and the intention of your heart pure—and let God enlarge your borders.

- **Lust Ruins Your Destiny:** "Ye ask, and receive not, because ye ask amiss, that ye may consume it upon your lusts." James 4:3 KJV. Maybe you "have not" because God knows that you want to consume your "ask" upon your lusts. Ask God to give you a clean heart. Ask God to renew your heart. Ask God to give you a heart that reflects His Way of doing things. "But seek ye first the kingdom of God, and his righteousness; and all these things shall be added unto you." Matthew 6:33 KJV.

In 2 Kings 4:13 AMPC, notice the Shunammite woman's response, even after Elisha had asked her what would she like in return, she answered, "I dwell among my own people [they are sufficient]." She was satisfied with her portion. She was satisfied with her life. She did not allow her "ask" to become an idol. She did not worship her "ask." She simply was honoring God by giving the man of God a place to dwell. Choose to worship God simply for who He is and not what He can do for you.

So let's examine what this Shunammite woman needed. 2 Kings 4:14 KJV declares, "And he said, What then is to be done for her? And Gehazi answered, Verily she hath no child, and her husband is old." Ah there's the need—she has no child. Her house had no legacy in place. Although she was considered great within the walls of the city—she had no successor. She had no heir.

Look at this powerful principle located in 2 Kings 4:14 KJV. Although the Shunammite woman had a "need," she did not let her need "lord" over her. Her need of an heir did not consume her. I'm pretty sure that it was discussed within the borders of their marriage, about the lack of a legacy. Although they lacked a son, they did not allow their "lack of legacy" to define them.

Married couples, don't allow your "need" to become your idol. Don't let that "thing" that you deeply desire to rule over your life, thoughts, marriage, and your actions. Keep your hands clean and your heart pure. Don't try to manipulate the circumstance in order to orchestrate what you need.

Matthew 6:8 KJV declares, "Be not ye therefore like unto them: for your Father knoweth what things ye have need of, before ye ask him." God knows what you have need of before you ask. Choose to trust God and walk forward in freedom.

Let's continue. 2 Kings 4:16 KJV declares, "And he said, About this season, according to the time of life, thou shalt embrace a son. And she said, Nay, my lord, thou man of God, do not lie unto thine handmaid." Notice the Shunammite woman's response to Elisha's declaration, she said, "Nay, my lord, thou man of God, do not lie unto thine handmaid." "Do not lie to me," she stated.

This heart-jerking response shows the "need" that was buried deep within the borders of her heart. Elisha had discovered the Shunammite woman's deep hidden desire. What's your "ask" that's buried deep within the borders of your heart? Surrender your "ask" to God. Surrender your heart to God. Seek Him, and don't let your "ask" become your idol. Don't let your "ask" rule your heart. "But seek ye first the kingdom of God, and his righteousness; and all these things shall be added unto you." Matthew 6:33 KJV.

Let's continue. 2 Kings 4:17 KJV declares, "And the woman conceived, and bare a son at that season that Elisha had said unto her, according to the time of life." And she conceived. She surrendered to the Word of the Lord. She obeyed God and reaped the fruit of submission and obedience.

2 Kings 4:17 AMPC expounds on it this way, "But the woman conceived and bore a son at that season the following year, as Elisha had said to her." Receive what God has declared over your life and you will conceive. Receive what God has declared over your marriage. Receive what God wants to do through your marriage. Receive what God wants to do through your family.

Don't idolize the promise—wait and worship God. Let God rewrite your story. "And so, after he had patiently endured, he obtained the promise." Hebrews 6:15 KJV.

## Day 21

# DECLARE LIFE

*Death and life are in the power of the tongue: and they that love it shall eat the fruit thereof.*

PROVERBS 18:21 KJV

The Bible declares that death and life are in the power of the tongue. Choose to tame your tongue and speak life over your family, life, and marriage. Choose to redirect your words and speak the Word of God over your marriage.

Proverbs 18:21 NLT declares, "The tongue can bring death or life; those who love to talk will reap the consequences." Choose to invest in your marriage. Shower and speak His Word over every aspect of your family, life, and marriage and you will have good success—God's success.

**Here are a few scriptures and daily declarations to speak over your life, your family, and over your marriage:**

- **Family Declaration: As for me and my house, we will serve the Lord.**

"And if it seem evil unto you to serve the Lord, choose you this day whom ye will serve; whether the gods which your fathers served that were on the other side of the flood, or the gods of the Amorites, in whose land ye dwell: but as for me and my house, we will serve the Lord." Joshua 24:15 KJV

- **We will obey and declare the Word of the Lord daily. We choose to walk in His Ways.**

    "This book of the law shall not depart out of thy mouth; but thou shalt meditate therein day and night, that thou mayest observe to do according to all that is written therein: for then thou shalt make thy way prosperous, and then thou shalt have good success. Have not I commanded thee? Be strong and of a good courage; be not afraid, neither be thou dismayed: for the Lord thy God is with thee whithersoever thou goest." Joshua 1:8-9 KJV.

- **Our family ways will please the Lord.**

    "When a man's ways please the Lord, he maketh even his enemies to be at peace with him." Proverbs 16:7 KJV

- **Father, remove our spiritual blinders and let us see Your Word clearly.**

    "And Jesus said unto him, Go thy way; thy faith hath made thee whole. And immediately he received his sight, and followed Jesus in the way." Mark 10:52 KJV

- **Our family shall live by faith.**

    "For therein is the righteousness of God revealed from faith to faith: as it is written, The just shall live by faith." Romans 1:17 KJV

- **We shall not stagger at Your Promises.**

    "He staggered not at the promise of God through unbelief; but was strong in faith, giving glory to God;" Romans 4:20 KJV

- **Though a thousand shall fall at our side and ten thousand at our right hand—it shall not come nigh unto us.**

"A thousand shall fall at thy side, and ten thousand at thy right hand; but it shall not come nigh thee." Psalms 91:7 KJV

- **Father, we will strengthen ourselves in You.**

"And David was greatly distressed; for the people spake of stoning him, because the soul of all the people was grieved, every man for his sons and for his daughters: but David encouraged himself in the Lord his God." 1 Samuel 30:6 KJV

- **Lord, our house will praise You for we are fearfully and wonderfully made.**

"I will praise thee; for I am fearfully and wonderfully made: marvellous are thy works; and that my soul knoweth right well." Psalms 139:14 KJV

- **Father, our mind is stable, and we are fixed on You. Lord, we will trust You.**

"A double minded man is unstable in all his ways." James 1:8 KJV

- **Father, our hands are diligent.**

"He becometh poor that dealeth with a slack hand: but the hand of the diligent maketh rich." Proverbs 10:4 KJV

- **Father God, in the Name of Jesus, our house will follow Your Word. Lord, our house will follow Your Voice.**

"And it shall come to pass, if thou shalt hearken diligently unto the voice of the Lord thy God, to observe and to do all his commandments which I command thee this day, that the Lord thy God will set thee on high above all nations of the earth: And all these blessings shall come on thee, and overtake thee, if thou shalt hearken unto the voice of the Lord thy God." Deuteronomy 28:1-2 KJV

- **Wealth and riches are in our house.**

  "Praise ye the Lord. Blessed is the man that feareth the Lord, that delighteth greatly in his commandments. His seed shall be mighty upon earth: the generation of the upright shall be blessed. Wealth and riches shall be in his house: and his righteousness endureth for ever." Psalms 112:1-3 KJV

- **Lord, send now prosperity.**

  "Save now, I beseech thee, O Lord: O Lord, I beseech thee, send now prosperity." Psalms 118:25 KJV

- **Wisdom dwells within the borders of our home. Witty ideas, inventions, and innovations dwell richly within the borders of our thoughts, our minds, and marriage.**

  "I wisdom dwell with prudence, and find out knowledge of witty inventions." Proverbs 8:12 KJV

- **It is the Lord who gives us power to get wealth.**

  "But thou shalt remember the Lord thy God: for it is he that giveth thee power to get wealth, that he may establish his covenant which he sware unto thy fathers, as it is this day." Deuteronomy 8:18 KJV

- **With long life, You shall satisfy us.**

  "With long life will I satisfy him, and shew him my salvation." Psalms 91:16 KJV

- **The Lord is the health of my countenance, and He is my God.**

  "Why art thou cast down, O my soul? and why art thou disquieted within me? hope thou in God: for I shall yet praise him, who is the health of my countenance, and my God." Psalms 42:11 KJV

- **We choose to honor the Lord with our substance.**

    "Honour the Lord with thy substance, and with the firstfruits of all thine increase: So shall thy barns be filled with plenty, and thy presses shall burst out with new wine." Proverbs 3:9-10 KJV

- **We are Tithers.**

    "Will a man rob God? Yet ye have robbed me. But ye say, Wherein have we robbed thee? In tithes and offerings. Ye are cursed with a curse: for ye have robbed me, even this whole nation. Bring ye all the tithes into the storehouse, that there may be meat in mine house, and prove me now herewith, saith the Lord of hosts, if I will not open you the windows of heaven, and pour you out a blessing, that there shall not be room enough to receive it. And I will rebuke the devourer for your sakes, and he shall not destroy the fruits of your ground; neither shall your vine cast her fruit before the time in the field, saith the Lord of hosts." Malachi 3:8-11 KJV

- **He makes our feet like hinds' feet and causes us to walk in high places.**

    "The Lord God is my strength, and he will make my feet like hinds' feet, and he will make me to walk upon mine high places." Habakkuk 3:19 KJV

- **Our house is built on Your Word.**

    "Therefore whosoever heareth these sayings of mine, and doeth them, I will liken him unto a wise man, which built his house upon a rock: And the rain descended, and the floods came, and the winds blew, and beat upon that house; and it fell not: for it was founded upon a rock. And every one that heareth these sayings of mine, and doeth them not, shall be likened unto a foolish man, which built his house upon the sand: And the rain descended, and the floods came, and the winds blew, and beat upon that house; and it fell: and great was the fall of it." Matthew 7:24-27 KJV

- **Blessed is the man that walketh not in the counsel of the ungodly.**

  "Blessed is the man that walketh not in the counsel of the ungodly, nor standeth in the way of sinners, nor sitteth in the seat of the scornful. But his delight is in the law of the Lord; and in his law doth he meditate day and night. And he shall be like a tree planted by the rivers of water, that bringeth forth his fruit in his season; his leaf also shall not wither; and whatsoever he doeth shall prosper." Psalms 1:1-3 KJV

- **The Lord will fight for us.**

  "The Lord shall fight for you, and ye shall hold your peace." Exodus 14:14 KJV

- **The Lord will give our house peace.**

  "The Lord lift up his countenance upon thee, and give thee peace." Numbers 6:26 KJV

- **His Peace covers our home.**

  "Wherefore say, Behold, I give unto him my covenant of peace:" Numbers 25:12 KJV

- **We shall live and not die.**

  "And the Lord said unto him, Peace be unto thee; fear not: thou shalt not die." Judges 6:23 KJV

- **His Peace rests in our house.**

"And thou shalt know that thy tabernacle shall be in peace; and thou shalt visit thy habitation, and shalt not sin." Job 5:24 KJV

- **The Lord will give us strength. His Peace is with us.**

  "The Lord will give strength unto his people; the Lord will bless his people with peace." Psalms 29:11 KJV

- **We choose to pursue Peace.**

  "Depart from evil, and do good; seek peace, and pursue it." Psalms 34:14 KJV

- **Great peace have they which love thy law.**

  "Great peace have they which love thy law: and nothing shall offend them." Psalms 119:165 KJV

- **His Peace dwells within our borders.**

  "Peace be within thy walls, and prosperity within thy palaces." Psalms 122:7 KJV

- **He fills our house with the finest of wheat.**

  "He maketh peace in thy borders, and filleth thee with the finest of the wheat." Psalms 147:14 KJV

- **Our hearts will forever keep Your Commandments.**

  "My son, forget not my law; but let thine heart keep my commandments: For length of days, and long life, and peace, shall they add to thee." Proverbs 3:1-2 KJV

# MY PRAYER FOR YOUR FAMILY AND MARRIAGE

Father God, in the Name of Jesus, I thank You for every couple who reads and clings to Your Word.

Father, I pray for the strength of these couples. Father, I declare that their marriages are blessed. Father, I declare that their hearts are pure and are softened toward You. Father, I declare that their ears will hear your Voice and another god they shall not follow.

Father, I declare, in the Name of Jesus, that they will serve no other idol. Lord, I declare that they will serve no other god.

Father, I declare, that this is a generation that seeks Your Face. Father, I declare, in the Name of Jesus, that their faith is strengthened as they move forward in You.

Father, I pray that the atmosphere of their home is blessed. Lord, let everything that their hands touch produce Your results. Lord, bless the ground of their marriage. Lord, bless the ground of their family.

Lord, I pray that Your Peace consumes the borders of their marriage. Father, I pray, that understanding flows. Father, I pray, that every exalted thing that's not like You is crushed.

Lord, I pray that their hearts surrender to You. Father, I declare, in the Name of Jesus, that generational bloodlines are shifted and transformed. Father, I pray that generational cycles are broken. Lord, I declare that their prayer life is strengthened in You.

Father, I pray that witty ideas, inventions, and insight flourishes within the borders of their home. Father, this generation surrenders to You. Lord, I declare that wealth and riches are in their house forever.

Father, I declare, in the Name of Jesus, that every form of witchcraft and manipulation are broken. I declare, in the Name of Jesus, that the Blood of Jesus covers their house and that their past is history and that their future is bright in You.

Lord, I thank You for my brother and my sister. Lead their footsteps. Lord, make their feet like hinds' feet and cause them to walk upon high places. Lord, stabilize their house. Father, enlarge them.

Lord, cause them to become successful. Father, cause them to prosper in every area of their family, life, and marriage.

Lord, guide their hearts. Father, lead their language. Father, guide their tongue. Father, rewrite the fabric, foundation, framework, history, and every aspect of their marriage.

In Jesus' Name. Amen.

FOR MORE BOOKS VISIT
www.VanceKJackson.com

www.ingramcontent.com/pod-product-compliance
Lightning Source LLC
Chambersburg PA
CBHW030910080526
44589CB00010B/239